_____

on

_____

by

_____

_____

"We are locked in a battle. This is not a friendly, gentleman's discussion. It is a life and death conflict between the spiritual hosts of wickedness and those who claim the name of Christ."
FRANCIS A. SCHAEFFER

SPIRIT*LED* PROMISES FOR

SPIRITUAL

WARFARE

PASSIO
THE ART OF AUTHENTIC FAITH

Most CHARISMA HOUSE BOOK GROUP products are available at special quantity discounts for bulk purchase for sales promotions, premiums, fund-raising, and educational needs. For details, write Charisma House Book Group, 600 Rinehart Road, Lake Mary, Florida 32746, or telephone (407) 333-0600.

SPIRITLED PROMISES FOR SPIRITUAL WARFARE
Published by Passio
Charisma Media/Charisma House Book Group
600 Rinehart Road
Lake Mary, Florida 32746
www.charismahouse.com

Cover design by Lisa Rae Cox
Design Director: Bill Johnson

Library of Congress Control Number: 2013914167
International Standard Book Number: 978-1-62136-578-5
E-book ISBN: 978-1-62136-606-5

First edition

13 14 15 16 17 — 987654321
Printed in the United States of America

"Many of us are hunting mice—while lions devour the land."

LEONARD RAVENHILL

Contents

    God's Favor...178

    God's Safety 179

    Garment of Righteousness................................180

    Delivered From Wickedness..............................181

    Warfare Prayers 183

    Arming for Victory 187

    Walking in God's Ways...................................196

    Demonic Spirits of Old and New Testaments............................198

INTRODUCTION

*The Church has to come together on its knees. The
people of God must repent and seek God's will
because the battle is a spiritual battle.*
—CHARLES COLSON

NOTHING IS MORE urgently important for all who
claim the name of *Christian* than to grasp and
understand the teachings from Scripture on spiritual warfare. From the very moment a person accepts Jesus as his
or her Savior and receives God's Holy Spirit, that person
is literally marked by the kingdom of darkness as an enemy.
We are at war with evil, a supernatural evil spearheaded by
Satan himself, and it is personal. Spiritual warfare affects
everyone. There are no retreat areas or safety zones where
you can exempt yourself from the battle.

The world today ridicules the spiritual realm. It is even
doubtful about the existence of God, it has no faith in Jesus
Christ, nor does it believe there are "principalities…and
powers…the rulers of the darkness of this world…spiri-
tual forces of evil in the heavenly places" (Eph. 6:12). We are
living in a perversely evil day. It is wicked in every respect. It
is so because evil and sin are so powerfully organized and so
deeply entrenched. The devil is unusually active, creating an
uncertainty about the essentials of faith.

Have you not felt, during some quiet time with God,

1

that you were going through a decisive battle that you've never experienced before? That battleground between the flesh and the Spirit is between the life of the Spirit and the fruit of the flesh. Though we walk in the flesh, Scripture teaches us we do not war according to the flesh. It is incumbent upon all Christians to realize that the weapons of this warfare are not human ~~weapons~~ fought in the flesh. They are instead spiritual weapons of truth and righteousness that tear down strongholds of an enemy who wages war in direct opposition to God, His kingdom, and His Word.

We are called to battle. We are called to warfare, a struggle. We must face this honestly. It's not enough to say, "Yes, I know the enemy is very strong, and I am weak." This is half the battle. Human willpower alone is not enough. We need to employ the power of God's Word—the whole armor of God—and then we will be able to stand. A spiritual battle must be fought in a spiritual manner with spiritual understanding. Our chief foe is Satan and his powers of darkness. Our weapons, therefore, cannot be of this world. Our weapons must be spiritual.

To be strong in the Lord you must remember the might of His power—the might of His strength. Do not be disheartened; do not be discouraged, confused, or misled. You may be standing alone, but you can still stand—enabled to fight evil while knowing the battle has already been won and God has equipped us with the promises of His Word. There is a place where God, through the power of the Holy Spirit, reigns supreme in our lives. The Spirit reveals this, preparing us to be more than a match for satanic forces.

It's a fight to the finish, with life and death hanging in the balance. Heaven or hell is literally at stake. This book presents a great weapon—the Word of God. It's a weapon that brings a sense of the presence of God, a reminder of His promises, and provides courage to the Christian. When the Lord calls you to become involved in spiritual warfare, you need to arm yourself with His Word, the promises that provide all Christians with the bold assurance they can be more than conquerors!

> Stand therefore, having your waist girded with truth, having put on the breastplate of righteousness.
>
> —Ephesians 6:14

"There's never a holiday in the spiritual realm... nothing but the full armor of God will ever suffice us in this terrible conflict in which we are engaged. There is no protection... against this wily, subtle, powerful enemy but the full armor of God himself."

C. S. LEWIS

Chapter 1

ESTABLISHING A FOUNDATION FOR WARFARE

BIBLICAL PROOF FOR ENGAGING IN WARFARE

For though we walk in the flesh, we do not war according to the flesh. For the weapons of our warfare are not carnal, but mighty through God to the pulling down of strongholds, casting down imaginations and every high thing that exalts itself against the knowledge of God, bringing every thought into captivity to the obedience of Christ.

—2 CORINTHIANS 10:3–5

And above all, taking the shield of faith, with which you will be able to extinguish all the fiery arrows of the evil one.

—EPHESIANS 6:16

How God anointed Jesus of Nazareth with the Holy Spirit and with power, who went about doing good and healing all who were oppressed by the devil, for God was with Him.

—ACTS 10:38

These signs will accompany those who believe: In My name they will cast out demons; they will speak with new tongues.

—MARK 16:17

But when the Spirit of truth comes, He will guide you into all truth. For He will not speak on His own authority. But

He will speak whatever He hears, and He will tell you things that are to come.

—John 16:13

Beloved, do not believe every spirit, but test the spirits to see whether they are from God, because many false prophets have gone out into the world. This is how you know the Spirit of God: Every spirit that confesses that Jesus Christ has come in the flesh is from God, and every spirit that does not confess that Jesus Christ has come in the flesh is not from God. This is the spirit of the antichrist, which you have heard is coming and is already in the world.

—1 John 4:1–3

You are of God, little children, and have overcome them, because He who is in you is greater than he who is in the world.

—1 John 4:4

Resist him firmly in the faith, knowing that the same afflictions are experienced by your brotherhood throughout the world.

—1 Peter 5:9

But the anointing which you have received from Him remains in you, and you do not need anyone to teach you. For as the same anointing teaches you concerning all things, and is truth, and is no lie, and just as it has taught you, remain in Him.

—1 John 2:27

Or else how can one enter a strong man's house and plunder his goods unless he first binds the strong man? And then he will plunder his house.

—MATTHEW 12:29

He called His twelve disciples to Him and gave them authority over unclean spirits, to cast them out, and to heal all kinds of sickness and all kinds of disease....As you go, preach saying, "The kingdom of heaven is at hand." Heal the sick, cleanse the lepers, raise the dead, and cast out demons. Freely you have received, freely give.

—MATTHEW 10:1, 7–8

"Now, look! The hand of the Lord is against you, and you shall be blind, not seeing the sun for a time." Immediately mist and darkness fell on him, and he went about seeking someone to lead him by the hand.

—ACTS 13:11

But you have an anointing from the Holy One, and you know all things.

—1 JOHN 2:20

The cords of death encircled me, and the pains of Sheol took hold of me; I found trouble and sorrow. Then called I upon the name of the LORD: "O LORD, I plead with You, deliver my soul." Gracious is the LORD and righteous; indeed, our God is merciful. The LORD protects the simple; I was brought low, and He helped me.

—PSALM 116:3–6

I pursued my enemies and overtook them; I did not return until they were destroyed. I wounded them, and they were not able to rise; they are fallen under my feet.

—Psalm 18:37–38

BATTLE SCRIPTURES

Your right hand, O Lord, is glorious in power. Your right hand, O Lord, shatters the enemy. In the greatness of Your excellence, You overthrow those who rise up against You. You send out Your wrath; it consumes them like stubble.

—Exodus 15:6–7

A man who is clean will gather the ashes of the heifer and deposit them outside the camp in a clean place, and it will be guarded for the assembly of the Israelites for water of purification. It is for purifying from sin.

—Numbers 19:9

Out of all your gifts you shall present every offering due to the Lord, from all the best of them, the consecrated part of them.

—Numbers 18:29

You must not be frightened of them, for the Lord your God is among you, a great and awesome God. The Lord your God will drive out those nations before you, little by little. You will not be able to destroy them all at once, lest the beasts of the field become too numerous for you. But the

LORD your God will deliver them to you and will throw them into a great confusion until they are destroyed.

—DEUTERONOMY 7:21–23

The eternal God is your refuge, and underneath you are the everlasting arms.

—DEUTERONOMY 33:27

The king said to Doeg, "You turn and fall upon the priests." And Doeg the Edomite turned and struck the priests and killed on that day eighty-five men who wore a linen ephod.

—1 SAMUEL 22:18

For if a man finds his enemy, will he let him safely go away? Therefore may the LORD reward you well for what you have done for me this day.

—1 SAMUEL 24:19

The men of David said to him, "This is the day of which the LORD said to you, 'I am giving your enemy into your hand. You may do with him as seems good in your eyes.'" Then David arose and secretly cut off the corner of Saul's robe.

—1 SAMUEL 24:4

If there is famine in the land, or if there is pestilence, blasting, mildew, locust, or caterpillar, if their enemies besiege them in the land of their cities, whatever plague, whatever sickness there be, whatever prayer and supplication is made by any man or by all of Your people Israel—each man knowing the plague of his own heart—and spread forth his hands toward this house, then may You hear in heaven, Your dwelling place, and forgive and give to every man according to his ways, whose hearts You know (for You, only You, know the hearts of all the children of men…).

—1 KINGS 8:37–39

For I was ashamed to ask the king for an escort of foot and horse soldiers to help us against the enemy on the way, because we had spoken to the king, saying, "The hand of our God is upon all who seek Him for good, but His power and His wrath are against all who forsake Him."

—EZRA 8:22

Then we began the journey from the Ahava River on the twelfth day of the first month to go to Jerusalem. The hand of our God was upon us, and He delivered us from the hand of the attacker and the ambusher along the way.

—EZRA 8:31

He has torn me in His wrath, and He has carried a grudge against me. He has gnashed me with His teeth; my enemy sharpens His gaze upon me. They have gaped upon me with their mouth; they have struck me upon the cheek with reproach; they have gathered themselves together against me.

—JOB 16:9–10

Surely you have spoken in my hearing, and I have heard the sound of your words saying, "I am clean, without transgression, I am innocent, nor is there iniquity in me."

—JOB 33:8–9

But may all those who seek refuge in You rejoice. May they ever shout for joy, because You defend them. May those who love Your name be joyful in You.

—Psalm 5:11

If I have repaid evil to him who was at peace with me, or have delivered my adversary without cause, then may the enemy pursue my life and overtake me; may my enemy trample my life to the ground, and lay my honor in the dust. Selah.

—Psalm 7:4–5

For You have maintained my right and my cause; You sat on the throne judging what is right. You have rebuked the nations, You have destroyed the wicked, You have wiped out their name forever and ever.

—Psalm 9:4–5

Take note and answer me, O Lord my God! Brighten my eyes, lest I sleep the sleep of death, lest my enemy say, "I have him," lest my foes exult when I stumble. I for my part confide in Your kindness. May my heart exult in Your salvation!

—Psalm 13:3–5

And have not delivered me up into the hand of the enemy; You have set my feet in a broad place.

—Psalm 31:8

May those who seek my life be ashamed and humiliated; may those who plan my injury be turned back and put to shame.

May they be as chaff before the wind, and may the angel of the Lord cast them down.

—Psalm 35:4–5

By this I know that You favor me, because my enemy does not triumph over me.

—Psalm 41:11

From the voice of him who reproaches and reviles, by reason of the enemy and avenger.

—Psalm 44:16

There they were in fear, where there was nothing to fear, for God has scattered the bones of him who camps against you; you have put them to shame, because God has rejected them.

—Psalm 53:5

For it was not an enemy who reproached me; then I could have endured it. Nor was it one who hated me who did great things against me; then I would have hid myself from him.

—Psalm 55:12

For You have been a refuge for me, and a strong tower from the enemy.

—Psalm 61:3

For I was envious at the boastful, I saw the prosperity of the wicked. For there are no pains in their death; their bodies are fat.

—Psalm 73:3–4

Give ear, O LORD, to my prayer, and attend to my plea for mercy. In the day of my trouble I will call upon You, for You will answer me.

—PSALM 86:6–7

But You, O Lord, are a God full of compassion and gracious, slow to anger, and abundant in mercy and truth. Turn to me and have mercy on me; give Your strength to Your servant, and save the humble son of Your female servant. Show me a sign of Your favor, that those who hate me may see it and be ashamed because You, LORD, have helped and comforted me.

—PSALM 86:15–17

Our fathers did not consider Your wonders in Egypt; they did not remember the greatness of Your mercy, but rebelled against Him at the sea, by the Red Sea. Nevertheless He saved them for His name's sake, that He might make His mighty power known. He rebuked the Red Sea, and it was dried up, so He led them through the depths as through the wilderness. He saved them from the hand of the one who hated them and redeemed them from the hand of the enemy.

—PSALM 106:7–10

Let the redeemed of the LORD speak out, whom He has redeemed from the hand of the enemy, and gathered them from foreign lands, from the east and from the west, from the north and from the south.

—PSALM 107:2–3

For the enemy has persecuted my soul, he has crushed my life down to the ground; he has made me to dwell in darkness, as those who have been long dead. Therefore my spirit is overwhelmed within me; my heart within me is desolate.

—Psalm 143:3–4

If your enemy is hungry, give him bread to eat; and if he is thirsty, give him water to drink; for you will heap coals of fire upon his head, and the Lord will reward you.

—Proverbs 25:21–22

Faithful are the wounds of a friend, but the kisses of an enemy are deceitful.

—Proverbs 27:6

Shall evil be recompensed for good? For they have dug a pit for my soul. Remember that I stood before you to speak good for them, and to turn away Your wrath from them. Therefore, deliver up their children to the famine and pour out their blood by the power of the sword; and let their wives be bereaved of their children and become widows. And let their men be put to death; let their young men be slain by the sword in battle.

—Jeremiah 18:20–21

I will scatter them before the enemy as with an east wind. I will show them the back and not the face in the day of their calamity.

—Jeremiah 18:17

Let a cry be heard from their houses, when You bring a troop suddenly upon them; for they have dug a pit to take me and hidden snares for my feet. Yet, LORD, You know all their counsel against me to slay me. Do not forgive their iniquity nor blot out their sin from Your sight. But let them be overthrown before You; deal thus with them in the time of Your anger.

—JEREMIAH 18:22–23

Proclaim this among the nations: Consecrate a war! Rouse the warriors! Let all the men of war draw near and rise. Beat your ploughshares into swords, and your pruning hooks into spears. Let the weakling say, "I am a warrior!"

—JOEL 3:9–10

Beware of false prophets who come to you in sheep's clothing, but inwardly they are ravenous wolves.

—MATTHEW 7:15

He told them another parable, saying, "The kingdom of heaven is like a man who sowed good seed in his field. But while men slept, his enemy came and sowed weeds among the wheat and went away."

—MATTHEW 13:24–25

His mercy is on those who fear Him from generation to generation. He has shown strength with His arm. He has scattered the proud in the imagination of their hearts. He has pulled down the mighty from their seats and exalted those of low degree.

—Luke 1:50–52

Look, I give you authority to trample on serpents and scorpions, and over all the power of the enemy. And nothing shall by any means hurt you.

—Luke 10:19

I am the vine, you are the branches. He who remains in Me, and I in him, bears much fruit. For without Me you can do nothing.

—John 15:5

Then Saul, who also is called Paul, filled with the Holy Spirit, stared at him and said, "You son of the devil, enemy of all righteousness, full of deceit and of all fraud, will you not cease perverting the right ways of the Lord?"

—Acts 13:9–10

If you then were raised with Christ, desire those things which are above, where Christ sits at the right hand of God. Set your affection on things above, not on things on earth. For you are dead, and your life is hidden with Christ in God.

—Colossians 3:1–3

Let your lives be without love of money, and be content with the things you have. For He has said, "I will never leave you, nor forsake you."

—Hebrews 13:5

Therefore submit yourselves to God. Resist the devil, and he will flee from you. Draw near to God, and He will draw near to you. Cleanse your hands, you sinners, and purify your hearts, you double minded.

—JAMES 4:7–8

This is the confidence that we have in Him, that if we ask anything according to His will, He hears us. So if we know that He hears whatever we ask, we know that we have whatever we asked of Him.

—1 JOHN 5:14–15

BATTLE FOR YOUR MIND

You will keep him in perfect peace, whose mind is stayed on You, because he trusts in You.

—ISAIAH 26:3

Pride goes before destruction, and a haughty spirit before a fall.

—PROVERBS 16:18

The sacrifice of the wicked is an abomination; how much more when he brings it with a wicked intent!

—PROVERBS 20:27

Beware of false prophets who come to you in sheep's clothing, but inwardly they are ravenous wolves.

—MATTHEW 7:15

Jesus answered them, "Take heed that no one deceives you."

—Matthew 24:4

The last enemy that will be destroyed is death.

—1 Corinthians 15:26

And many false prophets will rise and will deceive many.

—Matthew 24:11

He said to them, "Take heed what you hear. The measure you give will be measured for you, and to you who hear more will be given."

—Mark 4:24

Then Jesus said to those Jews who believed Him, "If you remain in My word, then you are truly My disciples."

—John 8:31

You shall know the truth, and the truth shall set you free.

—John 8:32

You are of your father the devil, and you want to do the desires of your father. He was a murderer from the beginning, and does not stand in the truth, because there is no truth in him. When he lies, he speaks from his own nature, for he is a liar and the father of lies.

—John 8:44

For if you live according to the flesh, you will die, but if through the Spirit you put to death the deeds of the body, you will live.

—Romans 8:13

No, in all these things we are more than conquerors through Him who loved us.

—ROMANS 8:37

Do not be conformed to this world, but be transformed by the renewing of your mind, that you may prove what is the good and acceptable and perfect will of God.

—ROMANS 12:2

For the weapons of our warfare are not carnal, but mighty through God to the pulling down of strongholds.

—2 CORINTHIANS 10:4

Casting down imaginations and every high thing that exalts itself against the knowledge of God, bringing every thought into captivity to the obedience of Christ.

—2 CORINTHIANS 10:5

Therefore this I say and testify in the Lord, that from now on you walk not as other Gentiles walk, in the vanity of their minds.

—EPHESIANS 4:17

Let no one deceive you with empty words, for because of these things the wrath of God is coming upon the sons of disobedience.

—EPHESIANS 5:6

Be anxious for nothing, but in everything, by prayer and sup-plication with gratitude, make your requests known to God. And the peace of God, which surpasses all understanding, will protect your hearts and minds through Christ Jesus. Finally, brothers, whatever things are true, whatever things are honest, whatever things are just, whatever things are pure, whatever things are lovely, whatever things are of good report, if there is any virtue, and if there is any praise, think on these things.

—PHILIPPIANS 4:6–8

He has delivered us from the power of darkness and has transferred us into the kingdom of His dear Son.

—COLOSSIANS 1:13

Do not let anyone cheat you of your reward by delighting in false humility and the worship of angels, dwelling on those things which he has not seen, vainly arrogant due to his unspiritual mind.

—COLOSSIANS 2:18

Set your affection on things above, not on things on earth.

—COLOSSIANS 3:2

Do not let anyone deceive you in any way. For that Day will not come unless a falling away comes first, and the man of sin is revealed, the son of destruction.

—2 THESSALONIANS 2:3

For God has not given us the spirit of fear, but of power, and love, and self-control.

—2 TIMOTHY 1:7

Let your lives be without love of money, and be content with the things you have. For He has said, "I will never leave you, nor forsake you."

—HEBREWS 13:5

Therefore submit yourselves to God. Resist the devil, and he will flee from you.

—JAMES 4:7

Who are protected by the power of God through faith for a salvation ready to be revealed in the last time.

—1 PETER 1:5

But there were also false prophets among the people, just as there will be false teachers among you, who will secretly bring in destructive heresies, even denying the Lord who bought them, bringing swift destruction upon themselves.

—2 PETER 2:1

Little children, let no one deceive you. The one who does righteousness is righteous, just as Christ is righteous.

—1 JOHN 3:7

Whoever has been born of God does not practice sin, for His seed remains in him. And he cannot keep on sinning, because he has been born of God.

—1 JOHN 3:9

WISDOM FOR THE BATTLE: CONFIDENCE

In whom we have boldness and confident access through faith in Him.

—EPHESIANS 3:12

They shall dwell safely in it and shall build houses and plant vineyards and dwell securely when I execute judgments on all those who despise them round about them. Then they shall know that I am the LORD their God.

—EZEKIEL 28:26

Therefore do not throw away your confidence, which will be greatly rewarded.

—HEBREWS 10:35

For thus says the Lord GOD, the Holy One of Israel, "In returning and rest you shall be saved. In quietness and in confidence shall be your strength." Yet you were not willing.

—ISAIAH 30:15

For the LORD will be your confidence, and will keep your foot from being caught.

—PROVERBS 3:26

Do not yield your members to sin as instruments of unrighteousness, but yield yourselves to God, as those who are alive from the dead, and your bodies to God as instruments of righteousness. For sin shall not have dominion over you, for you are not under the law, but under grace.

—ROMANS 6:13–14

WISDOM FOR THE BATTLE: GUIDANCE

And he sought after God in the days of Zechariah, the one who instructed him in the fear of the LORD. And in the days that he sought after the LORD, God caused him to succeed.

—2 CHRONICLES 26:5

These words, which I am commanding you today, shall be in your heart. You shall teach them diligently to your children and shall talk of them when you sit in your house, and when you walk by the way and when you lie down and when you rise up. You shall bind them as a sign on your hand, and they shall be as frontlets between your eyes. You shall write them on the doorposts of your house and on your gates.

—DEUTERONOMY 6:6–9

If an iron piece is blunt and there is no one to sharpen it, then he must prevail with more strength. Wisdom is a benefit to succeed.

—ECCLESIASTES 10:10

For the protective shadow of wisdom is like the protective shadow of silver, and the advantage of knowledge is that having wisdom preserves the life of the one who possesses it.

—ECCLESIASTES 7:12

The voice of him who cries out, "Prepare the way of the LORD in the wilderness, make straight in the desert a highway for our God. Let every valley be lifted up, and every mountain and hill be made low, and let the rough ground become a plain, and the rugged places a broad valley."

—Isaiah 40:3–4

"I have raised him up in righteousness, and I will direct all his ways. He shall build My city, and he shall let My captives go, neither for price nor reward," says the Lord of Hosts.

—Isaiah 45:13

But when the Spirit of truth comes, He will guide you into all truth. For He will not speak on His own authority. But He will speak whatever He hears, and He will tell you things that are to come.

—John 16:13

But He said, "Indeed, blessed are those who hear the word of God and keep it."

—Luke 11:28

A man's heart devises his way, but the Lord directs his steps.

—Proverbs 16:9

Through wisdom is a house built, and by understanding it is established.

—Proverbs 24:3

Happy is the man who finds wisdom, and the man who gets understanding.

—Proverbs 3:13

But the path of the just is as the shining light, that shines more and more unto the perfect day.

—Proverbs 4:18

The law of the Lord is perfect, converting the soul. The testimony of the Lord is sure, making wise the simple.

—Psalm 19:7

You are my hiding place; You will preserve me from trouble; You will surround me with shouts of deliverance. Selah. I will instruct you and teach you in the way which you will go; I will counsel you with my eye on you.

—Psalm 32:7–8

You will guide me with Your counsel, and afterward receive me to glory.

—Psalm 73:24

To fulfill what was spoken by the prophet: "I will open My mouth in parables. I will say things which have been kept secret since the foundation of the world."

—Matthew 13:35

Wisdom for the Battle: Understanding

But we speak the wisdom of God in a mystery, the hidden wisdom, which God ordained before the ages for our glory.

—1 Corinthians 2:7

Doubtless, it is not profitable for me to boast. So I will move on to visions and revelations of the Lord.

—2 Corinthians 12:1

Immediately, something like scales fell from his eyes, and he could see again. And he rose up and was baptized.

—Acts 9:18

But there is a God in heaven who reveals secrets and makes known to King Nebuchadnezzar what shall be in the latter days. Your dream and the visions of your head upon your bed are these.

—Daniel 2:28

The secret things belong to the Lord our God, but those things which are revealed belong to us and to our children forever, so that we may keep all the words of this law.

—Deuteronomy 29:29

Then God responded to Solomon, "Because this was in your heart and you did not ask for possessions, wealth, and honor, or even the life of those who hate you, nor have you asked for many days of life, but you have asked Me for wisdom and knowledge that you might govern My people over whom I have made you king, wisdom and knowledge are now given to you. Possessions, wealth, and honor I will also give to you, such has not been given to kings before you nor those who will follow after you."

—2 Chronicles 1:11–12

To understand a proverb and the interpretation, the words of the wise and their riddles.

—PROVERBS 1:6

Open my eyes, that I may behold wondrous things from Your law.

—PSALM 119:18

Giving thanks to the Father, who has enabled us to be partakers in the inheritance of the saints in light. He has delivered us from the power of darkness and has transferred us into the kingdom of His dear Son, in whom we have redemption through His blood, the forgiveness of sins.

—COLOSSIANS 1:12–14

Let the word of Christ dwell in you richly in all wisdom, teaching and admonishing one another in psalms and hymns and spiritual songs, singing with grace in your hearts to the Lord. And whatever you do in word or deed, do all in the name of the Lord Jesus, giving thanks to God the Father through Him.

—COLOSSIANS 3:16–17

WHO WE ARE IN CHRIST

Now these are the commandments, the statutes, and the ordinances which the LORD your God commanded to teach you, so that you may observe them in the land which you are crossing over to possess, so that you might fear the LORD your God in order to keep all His statutes and His commandments which I command you—you, and your son, and your grandson—all the days of your life, so that your days may be prolonged. Hear therefore, O Israel, and be careful to do it, so that it may be well with you and so that you may multiply greatly, as the LORD the God of your fathers has promised you in the land that flows with milk and honey.

—DEUTERONOMY 6:1–3

You have placed gladness in my heart. That is better than when their corn and their new wine abound.

—PSALM 4:7

The fear of the LORD is clean, enduring forever. The judgments of the LORD are true and righteous altogether. More to be desired are they than gold, yes, than much fine gold; sweeter also than honey and the honeycomb.

—PSALM 19:9–10

Lift up your heads, O you gates; and be lifted up, you everlasting doors, that the King of glory may enter.

—PSALM 24:7

To You, O LORD will I cry; my Rock, do not be silent to me; lest if You were silent to me, then I would become like those who go down to the pit. Hear the voice of my supplications when I cry to You, when I lift up my hands toward Your most holy place.

—PSALM 28:1–2

I will sing of the mercies of the LORD forever; with my mouth I will make known Your faithfulness to all generations.... Your offspring I will establish forever, and build up your throne for all generations.

—PSALM 89:1, 4

Bless the LORD, you His angels, who are mighty, and do His commands, and obey the voice of His word. Bless the LORD, all you His hosts; you servants who do His pleasure. Bless the LORD, all His works in all places of His dominion. Bless the LORD, O my soul!

—PSALM 103:20–22

You who fear the LORD, trust in the LORD; He is their help and their shield.

—PSALM 115:11

To make known to people His mighty acts, and the glorious majesty of His kingdom.

—PSALM 145:12

The fear of the LORD tends to life, and he who has it will abide satisfied; he will not be visited with evil.

—PROVERBS 19:23

Look, I am sending you out as sheep in the midst of wolves. Therefore be wise as serpents and harmless as doves.

—MATTHEW 10:16

He who has My commandments and keeps them is the one who loves Me. And he who loves Me will be loved by My Father. And I will love him and will reveal Myself to him.

—John 14:21

If a man does not remain in Me, he is thrown out as a branch and withers. And they gather them and throw them into the fire, and they are burned. If you remain in Me, and My words remain in you, you will ask whatever you desire, and it shall be done for you.

—John 15:6–7

Now thanks be to God who always causes us to triumph in Christ and through us reveals the fragrance of His knowledge in every place.

—2 Corinthians 2:14

We have such trust through Christ toward God, not that we are sufficient in ourselves to take credit for anything of ourselves, but our sufficiency is from God.

—2 Corinthians 3:4–5

For God, who commanded the light to shine out of darkness, has shone in our hearts to give the light of the knowledge of the glory of God in the face of Jesus Christ.

—2 Corinthians 4:6

Casting down imaginations and every high thing that exalts itself against the knowledge of God, bringing every thought into captivity to the obedience of Christ, and being ready to punish all disobedience when your obedience is complete.

—2 Corinthians 10:5–6

Blessed be the God and Father of our Lord Jesus Christ, who has blessed us with every spiritual blessing in the heavenly places in Christ. Just as He chose us in Him before the foundation of the world, to be holy and blameless before Him in love.

—Ephesians 1:3–4

In Him you also, after hearing the word of truth, the gospel of your salvation, and after believing in Him, were sealed with the promised Holy Spirit, who is the guarantee of our inheritance until the redemption of the purchased possession, to the praise of His glory.

—Ephesians 1:13–14

So we may no longer be children, tossed here and there by waves and carried about with every wind of doctrine by the trickery of men, by craftiness with deceitful scheming. But, speaking the truth in love, we may grow up in all things into Him, who is the head, Christ Himself, from whom the whole body is joined together and connected by every joint and ligament, as every part effectively does its work and grows, building itself up in love.

—Ephesians 4:14–16

The Spirit Himself bears witness with our spirits that we are the children of God, and if children, then heirs: heirs of God and joint-heirs with Christ, if indeed we suffer with Him, that we may also be glorified with Him.

—Romans 8:16–17

Now I urge you, brothers, to closely watch those who cause divisions and offenses, contrary to the teaching which you have learned, and avoid them. For such people do not serve our Lord Jesus Christ, but their own appetites, and through smooth talk and flattery they deceive the hearts of the unsuspecting.

—Romans 16:17–18

All Scripture is inspired by God and is profitable for teaching, for reproof, for correction, and for instruction in righteousness, that the man of God may be complete, thoroughly equipped for every good work.

—2 Timothy 3:16–17

"*The reason why many fail in battle is because they wait until the hour of battle. The reason why others succeed is because they have gained their victory on their knees long before the battle came.... Anticipate your battles; fight them on your knees before temptation comes, and you will always have victory.*"

R. A. Torrey

Chapter 2

BREAKING THROUGH OPPOSITION

OUR COVENANT WITH GOD

Your covenant with death shall be annulled, and your agreement with hell shall not stand. When the overflowing scourge passes through, then you shall be trodden down by it.

—ISAIAH 28:18

You must not be frightened of them, for the LORD your God is among you, a great and awesome God. The LORD your God will drive out those nations before you, little by little. You will not be able to destroy them all at once, lest the beasts of the field become too numerous for you. But the LORD your God will deliver them to you and will throw them into a great confusion until they are destroyed. He will deliver their kings into your hand so that you may erase their names from under heaven. No man will be able to stand before you until you have destroyed them.

—DEUTERONOMY 7:21–24

Let us draw near with a true heart in full assurance of faith, having our hearts sprinkled to cleanse them from an evil conscience, and our bodies washed with pure water. Let us firmly hold the profession of our faith without wavering, for

He who promised is faithful. And let us consider how to spur one another to love and to good works.

—HEBREWS 10:22–24

As it is appointed for men to die once, but after this comes the judgment, so Christ was offered once to bear the sins of many, and He will appear a second time, not to bear sin but to save those who eagerly wait for Him.

—HEBREWS 9:27–28

If we confess our sins, He is faithful and just to forgive us our sins and cleanse us from all unrighteousness. If we say that we have not sinned, we make Him a liar and His word is not in us.

—1 JOHN 1:9–10

CLAIMING YOUR BREAKTHROUGH

Then your light shall break forth as the morning, and your recovery shall spring forth speedily, and your righteousness shall go before you. The glory of the LORD shall be your reward.

—ISAIAH 58:8

The Spirit of the Lord GOD is upon Me because the LORD has anointed Me to preach good news to the poor. He has sent Me to heal the brokenhearted, to proclaim liberty to the captives, and the opening of the prison to those who are bound.

—ISAIAH 61:1

He who breaks through has gone up before them. They will break through and pass the gate and go out by it. Then their king will pass on before them, the LORD at their head.

—MICAH 2:13

For we are not commending ourselves again to you. Instead, we give you occasion to boast on our behalf, that you may have something to answer those who boast in appearance and not in heart.

—2 CORINTHIANS 5:12

The end of all things is near. Therefore be solemn and sober so you can pray.

—1 PETER 4:7

BREAKING THE CURSE OF DEATH

Trust in the LORD, and do good; dwell in the land and practice faithfulness.

—PSALM 37:3

For yet a little while, and the wicked will not be; you will look diligently for their place, and it will not be.

—PSALM 37:10

The wicked plot against the righteous, and grind their teeth against them. The Lord will laugh at him, for He sees that his day is coming.

—PSALM 37:12–13

"Thus shall they know that I, the LORD their God, am with them, and that they, the house of Israel, are My people," says the Lord GOD. "As for you, My flock, the flock of My pasture, you are men, and I am your God," says the Lord GOD.

—EZEKIEL 34:30–31

The LORD is good, a stronghold in the day of distress; and He knows those who take refuge in Him.

—NAHUM 1:7

BREAKING GENERATIONAL CURSES

Then God said, "This is the sign of the covenant which I am making between Me and you and every living creature that is with you, for all future generations."

—GENESIS 9:12

I will set your boundaries from the Red Sea to the sea of the Philistines, and from the desert to the River; for I will deliver the inhabitants of the land into your hand, and you will drive them out before you. You must not make a covenant with them or with their gods. They shall not live in your land, lest they cause you to sin against Me, for if you serve their gods, it will surely be a snare to you.

—EXODUS 23:31–33

Thus says the LORD, I am bringing disaster on this place and all who dwell in it, even all the curses that are written in the book that they read before the king of Judah.

—2 CHRONICLES 34:24

I the LORD have called You in righteousness, and will hold Your hand, and will keep You, and appoint You for a covenant of the people, for a light of the Gentiles.

—Isaiah 42:6

But they rebelled and grieved His Holy Spirit. Therefore, He turned Himself to be their enemy, and He fought against them.

—Isaiah 63:10

Again, you have heard that it was said by the ancients, "You shall not swear falsely, but shall fulfill your oaths to the Lord."

—Matthew 5:33

Jesus went throughout all the cities and villages, teaching in their synagogues, preaching the gospel of the kingdom, and healing every sickness and every disease among the people.

—Matthew 9:35

Therefore if the Son sets you free, you shall be free indeed.

—John 8:36

You stiff-necked people, uncircumcised in heart and ears! You always resist the Holy Spirit. As your fathers did, so do you.

—Acts 7:51

Follow the pattern of sound teaching which you have heard from me in the faith and love that is in Christ Jesus.

—2 Timothy 1:13

PERSEVERANCE IN ADVERSITY

Many are the afflictions of the righteous, but the LORD delivers him out of them all.

—PSALM 34:19

Though he falls, he will not be hurled down, for the LORD supports him with His hand.

—PSALM 37:24

Before I was afflicted I wandered, but now I keep Your word.

—PSALM 119:67

See, I have refined you, but not with silver. I have chosen you in the furnace of affliction.

—ISAIAH 48:10

For a small moment I have forsaken you, but with great mercies I will gather you.

—ISAIAH 54:7

Do not rejoice over me, my enemy! Although I have fallen, I will rise. Although I dwell in darkness, the LORD is my light!

—MICAH 7:8

In your endurance you will gain your souls.

—LUKE 21:19

Not only so, but we also boast in tribulation, knowing that tribulation produces patience, patience produces character, and character produces hope. And hope does not disappoint, because the love of God is shed abroad in our hearts by the Holy Spirit who has been given to us.

—Romans 5:3–5

For I consider that the sufferings of this present time are not worthy to be compared with the glory which shall be revealed to us.

—Romans 8:18

We know that all things work together for good to those who love God, to those who are called according to His purpose.

—Romans 8:28

My brothers, count it all joy when you fall into diverse temptations, knowing that the trying of your faith develops patience. But let patience perfect its work, that you may be perfect and complete, lacking nothing.

—James 1:2–4

Keep your tongue from evil, and your lips from speaking deceit. Turn away from evil, and do good; seek peace, and pursue it.

—Psalm 34:13–14

I have spoken these things to you while I am still with you. But the Counselor, the Holy Spirit, whom the Father will send in My name, will teach you everything and remind you of all that I told you.

—John 14:25–26

That you may walk in a manner worthy of the Lord, pleasing to all, being fruitful in every good work, and increasing in the knowledge of God.

—Colossians 1:10

He is before all things, and in Him all things hold together.

—Colossians 1:17

Therefore, brothers, we have confidence to enter the Most Holy Place by the blood of Jesus, by a new and living way that He has opened for us through the veil, that is to say, His flesh.

—Hebrews 10:19–20

This then is the message which we have heard from Him and declare to you: God is light, and in Him is no darkness at all. If we say that we have fellowship with Him, yet walk in darkness, we lie and do not practice the truth. But if we walk in the light as He is in the light, we have fellowship one with another, and the blood of Jesus Christ His Son cleanses us from all sin.

—1 John 1:5–7

RELEASING SPOILERS

Who leads counselors away stripped, and makes fools of judges.... Who leads away priests stripped, and overthrows the mighty.

—Job 12:17, 19

Woe to you, O destroyer, though you were not destroyed, and he who is treacherous though others did not deal treacherously with you! When you cease destroying, you shall be destroyed. And when you finish dealing treacherously, others shall deal treacherously with you.

—Isaiah 33:1

The destroyers have come upon all high places through the wilderness, for the sword of the Lord shall devour from the one end of the land even to the other end of the land. No one shall have peace.

—Jeremiah 12:12

Therefore a tumult will arise among your people, and all your fortresses will be destroyed, as Shalman destroyed Beth-arbel in the day of battle—mothers were dashed to pieces upon their children.

—Hosea 10:14

There is the sound of wailing shepherds, because their glory is ruined. There is the sound of roaring lions, because the pride of Jordan is ruined.

—Zechariah 11:3

But when a stronger man than he attacks and overpowers him, he seizes all the armor in which the man trusted and divides his spoils.

—Luke 11:22

SPEAKING TO MOUNTAINS

See, I will make you a new sharp threshing instrument with double edges. You shall thresh the mountains, and beat them small, and shall make the hills as chaff.

—ISAIAH 41:15

I will lay waste mountains and hills and dry up all their vegetation. And I will make the rivers islands, and I will dry up the pools.

—ISAIAH 42:15

He puts forth his hand upon the rock; He overturns the mountains by the roots.

—JOB 28:9

The mountains quaked before the LORD, this very Sinai, before the LORD God of Israel.

—JUDGES 5:5

Therefore, O mountains of Israel, hear the word of the Lord GOD. "Thus says the Lord GOD to the mountains and to the hills, to the rivers and to the valleys, to the desolate wastes and to the cities that are forsaken, which became a prey and derision to the rest of the nations that are round about."

—EZEKIEL 36:4

Listen to what the LORD says: "Arise, plead your case before the mountains, that the hills may hear your voice."

—MICAH 6:1

Hear, mountains, the indictment of the LORD, O enduring foundations of the earth—that the LORD has an indictment against His people, and against Israel He will dispute.

—MICAH 6:2

The mountains saw You and trembled; the overflowing water passed by. The deep lifted its voice, and lifted its hands on high.

—HABAKKUK 3:10

"I am against you, O destroying mountain," says the LORD, "who destroys all the earth. And I will stretch out My hand against you, and roll you down from the rocks, and will make you a burnt mountain."

—JEREMIAH 51:25

Who are you, O great mountain? Before Zerubbabel you will be made level ground, and he will bring out the chief stone amidst shouting of "Grace! Grace to the stone!"

—ZECHARIAH 4:7

STANDING YOUR GROUND

For You are not a God who has pleasure in wickedness, nor will evil dwell with You. Those who boast will not stand in Your sight. You hate all workers of iniquity. You will destroy those who speak lies. The LORD abhors one who is guilty of bloodshed and treachery.

—PSALM 5:4–6

Do not fret because of evildoers, nor be jealous of those who do injustice. For they will quickly wither like the grass, and fade like the green herbs.

—PSALM 37:1–2

Let the heavens praise Your wonders, O LORD, and Your faithfulness in the assembly of the divine holy ones.

—PSALM 89:5

These six things the LORD hates, yes, seven are an abomination to him: a proud look, a lying tongue, and hands that shed innocent blood, a heart that devises wicked imaginations, feet that are swift in running to mischief, a false witness who speaks lies, and he who sows discord among brethren.

—PROVERBS 6:16–19

There will no evil happen to the just, but the wicked will be filled with mischief.

—PROVERBS 12:21

Call to Me, and I will answer you, and I will tell you great and mysterious things you did not know.

—JEREMIAH 33:3

It is of the LORD's mercies that we are not consumed, because His compassions do not fail. They are new every morning. Great is Your faithfulness.

—LAMENTATIONS 3:22–23

"At that time I will bring you in, at the time when I gather you; for I will make you renowned and praised among all peoples of the earth, when I restore your fortunes before your eyes," says the LORD.

—ZEPHANIAH 3:20

For thus says the LORD of Hosts, "Once more, in a little while, I will shake the heavens and earth, the sea and dry land. And I will shake all the nations, and they will come with the wealth of all nations, and I will fill this house with glory," says the LORD of Hosts.

—HAGGAI 2:6–7

Or else how can one enter a strong man's house and plunder his goods unless he first binds the strong man? And then he will plunder his house.

—MATTHEW 12:29

So that now the manifold wisdom of God might be made known by the church to the principalities and powers in the heavenly places.

—EPHESIANS 3:10

Finally, my brothers, be strong in the Lord and in the power of His might.

—EPHESIANS 6:10

So then, as the children share in flesh and blood, He likewise took part in these, so that through death He might destroy him who has the power of death, that is, the devil, and deliver those who through fear of death were throughout their lives subject to bondage.

—HEBREWS 2:14–15

Is anyone among you suffering? Let him pray. Is anyone merry? Let him sing psalms.

—James 5:13

But rejoice in so far as you share in Christ's sufferings, so that you may rejoice and be glad also in the revelation of His glory.

—1 Peter 4:13

Chapter 3

UNDERSTANDING DELIVERANCE

DELIVERANCE

But the worthless individual is like a thorn tossed away, all of them, for they cannot be taken with the hand; but the one who touches them must have an iron implement and the shaft of a spear, and they must be burned with fire on the spot.

—2 Samuel 23:6–7

With the kind You will show Yourself kind; with an upright person You will show Yourself upright.

—Psalm 18:25

For You will cause my lamp to shine; the Lord my God will enlighten my darkness. For by You I can run through a troop, and by my God I can leap a wall.

—Psalm 18:28–29

I sought the Lord, and He answered me, and delivered me from all my fears.

—Psalm 34:4

The Lord redeems the life of His servants, and all who take refuge in Him will not be punished.

—Psalm 34:22

The LORD is merciful and gracious, slow to anger, and abounding in mercy.

—PSALM 103:8

But the mercy of the LORD is from everlasting to everlasting upon those who fear Him, and His righteousness to children's children, to those who keep His covenant, and to those who remember to do His commandments.

—PSALM 103:17–18

Awake, awake! Put on your strength, O Zion. Put on your beautiful garments, O Jerusalem, the holy city. For the uncircumcised and the unclean will no longer enter you. Shake yourself from the dust. Arise, O captive Jerusalem. Loose yourself from the bonds of your neck, O captive daughter of Zion.

—ISAIAH 52:1–2

Then Paul and Barnabas boldly said, "It was necessary that the word of God should be spoken to you first. But seeing you reject it, and judge yourselves unworthy of eternal life, we are turning to the Gentiles. For thus has the Lord commanded us, 'I have established you to be a light of the Gentiles, that you may bring salvation to the ends of the earth.'"

—ACTS 13:46–47

And a great many of the brothers in the Lord, having become confident because of my incarcerations, have dared to speak the word without fear.

—PHILIPPIANS 1:14

Activate Your Faith

And she was bitter, and prayed to the Lord, and wept severely. So she made a vow and said, "O Lord of Hosts, if You will indeed look on the affliction of Your maidservant, and remember me and not forget Your maidservant, but will give to Your maidservant a baby boy, then I will give him to the Lord all the days of his life and no razor will ever come upon his head."

—1 Samuel 1:10–11

"By creating the fruit of the lips. Peace, peace to him who is far off and to him who is near," says the Lord, "and I will heal him."

—Isaiah 57:19

"For I will restore you to health; I will heal you of your wounds," says the Lord. "For they called you an outcast, saying, 'This is Zion whom no one cares for.'"

—Jeremiah 30:17

When she had heard of Jesus, she came in the crowd behind Him and touched His garment. For she said, "If I may touch His garments, I shall be healed."

—Mark 5:27–28

The apostles said to the Lord, "Increase our faith." The Lord said, "If you had faith as a grain of mustard seed, you could say to this mulberry tree, 'Be uprooted and be planted in the sea,' and it would obey you."

—Luke 17:5–6

Deliverance From Anger, Bitterness, and Unforgiveness

Let go of anger, and forsake wrath; do not fret—it surely leads to evil deeds. For evildoers will be cut off, but those who hope in the Lord will inherit the earth.

—Psalm 37:8–9

A soft answer turns away wrath, but grievous words stir up anger.

—Proverbs 15:1

They will lick dust like the serpent, like crawling creatures of the earth. They will come shuddering from their lairs. They will turn in dread to the Lord our God, and they will be afraid of you. Who is a God like You, bearing iniquity and passing over transgression for the remnant of His inheritance? He does not remain angry forever, because He delights in benevolence.

—Micah 7:17–18

So on the contrary, you ought to forgive him and comfort him, lest perhaps he might be swallowed up with excessive sorrow. Therefore I ask you to confirm your love toward him. For to this end I also wrote, so that I might know that you are proving yourselves by whether you are being obedient in all things. Whomever you forgive anything, I also forgive. For if I forgave someone anything, for your sakes I forgave it in Christ.

—2 Corinthians 2:7–10

Watching diligently so that no one falls short of the grace of God, lest any root of bitterness spring up to cause trouble, and many become defiled by it.

—Hebrews 12:15

DELIVERANCE FROM ENEMIES

Say to God, "How awesome are Your works!" Through the greatness of Your power Your enemies cringe before You.

—Psalm 66:3

Show me a sign of Your favor, that those who hate me may see it and be ashamed because You, Lord, have helped and comforted me.

—Psalm 86:17

The light of Israel shall be a fire, and his Holy One a flame. And it shall burn and devour his thorns and his briers in one day.

—Isaiah 10:17

The Lord of Hosts has sworn saying, "Surely as I have thought, so it shall come to pass. And as I have purposed, so it shall stand. That I will break the Assyrian in My land, and on My mountains tread him under foot. Then shall his yoke depart from off them and his burden depart from off their shoulders. This is the purpose that is purposed on the whole earth. And this is the hand that is stretched out on all the nations."

—Isaiah 14:24–26

"Surely the day is coming, burning like an oven; all the proud, yes, all evildoers will be stubble. The day that is coming will burn them up," says the LORD of Hosts, "so that it will leave them neither root nor branch."

—MALACHI 4:1

REBUKING THE ENEMY

Rebuke the animals that live among the reeds, the herd of bulls, with the calves of the people, until everyone submits himself with pieces of silver; scatter peoples who delight in war.

—PSALM 68:30

At Your rebuke they fled; at the sound of Your thunder they departed away.

—PSALM 104:7

He rebuked the Red Sea, and it was dried up, so He led them through the depths as through the wilderness.

—PSALM 106:9

You have rebuked the proud, those cursed, who depart from Your commandments.

—PSALM 119:21

For the LORD shall come with fire and with His chariots like a whirlwind, to render His anger with fury and His rebuke with flames of fire.

—ISAIAH 66:15

The nations rumble like the rumbling of many waters. But God shall rebuke them, and they shall flee far off, and shall be chased as the chaff of the mountains before the wind, and like rolling dust before the whirlwind.

—Isaiah 17:13

I will execute great vengeance upon them with furious rebukes. And they shall know that I am the Lord when I lay My vengeance upon them.

—Ezekiel 25:17

Jesus rebuked him, saying, "Be silent and come out of him!"

—Mark 1:25

He rose and rebuked the wind, and said to the sea, "Peace, be still!" Then the wind ceased and there was a great calm.

—Mark 4:39

While he was coming, the demon threw him down and convulsed him. But Jesus rebuked the unclean spirit, and healed the child, and returned him to his father.

—Luke 9:42

STANDING AGAINST SATAN

Then Jesus said to him, "Get away from here, Satan! For it is written, 'You shall worship the Lord your God, and Him only shall you serve.'"

—Matthew 4:10

Then should not this woman, being a daughter of Abraham whom Satan has bound these eighteen years, be loosed from this bondage on the Sabbath?

—LUKE 13:16

Then the Lord said, "Simon, Simon, listen! Satan has demanded to have you to sift you as wheat."

—LUKE 22:31

Do not give place to the devil.

—EPHESIANS 4:27

Be sober and watchful, because your adversary the devil walks around as a roaring lion, seeking whom he may devour. Resist him firmly in the faith, knowing that the same afflictions are experienced by your brotherhood throughout the world.

—1 PETER 5:8–9

I know your works and where you live, where Satan's throne is. Yet you hold firmly to My name, and did not deny My faith even in the days of Antipas, My faithful martyr, who was killed among you, where Satan dwells.

—REVELATION 2:13

Let God arise, let His enemies be scattered; let those who hate Him flee before Him.

—PSALM 68:1

You are of your father the devil, and you want to do the desires of your father. He was a murderer from the beginning, and does not stand in the truth, because there is no truth in him. When he lies, he speaks from his own nature, for he is a liar and the father of lies.

—John 8: 44

Lest Satan should take advantage of us. For we are not ignorant of his devices.

—2 Corinthians 2:11

And no wonder! For even Satan disguises himself as an angel of light.

—2 Corinthians 11:14

Therefore submit yourselves to God. Resist the devil, and he will flee from you.

—James 4:7

WITCHCRAFT AND THE OCCULT

But this is how you shall deal with them: You shall destroy their altars and break down their images and cut down their Asherim and burn their graven images with fire. For you are a holy people to the Lord your God. The Lord your God has chosen you to be His special people, treasured above all peoples who are on the face of the earth.

—Deuteronomy 7:5–6

There must not be found among you anyone who makes his son or his daughter pass through the fire, or who uses divination, or uses witchcraft, or an interpreter of omens, or a sorcerer, or one who casts spells, or a spiritualist, or an occultist,

or a necromancer. For all that do these things are an abomination to the Lord, and because of these abominations the
Lord your God will drive them out from before you.

—Deuteronomy 18:10–12

When I and all who are with me blow the horn, then you
will blow the horns all around the camp and shout, "For the
Lord and for Gideon!"

—Judges 7:18

The people sacrificed on mountain tops, because no house
had yet been built for the name of the Lord.

—1 Kings 3:2

He built shrines on the mountain tops and made priests from
all the people, even those who were not of the tribe of Levi.

—1 Kings 12:31

But the high places were not all removed, even though Asa's
heart was wholly devoted to the Lord all his days.

—1 Kings 15:14

When Joram saw Jehu he said, "Is it peace, Jehu?" And he
said, "What peace, so long as the harlotries of your mother
Jezebel and her sorceries are so many?"

—2 Kings 9:22

Moreover all the houses of the high places that were in the
cities of Samaria, which the kings of Israel had made to

provoke the Lord to anger, Josiah removed. He did to them just as he had done in Bethel.

—2 Kings 23:19

He took down the foreign altars and high places, and he shattered the pillars and cut down the Asherim poles.

—2 Chronicles 14:3

He even made sacrifices and offered incense on the high places of the hills and under every green tree.

—2 Chronicles 28:4

Then in every city in Judah he made high places to make offerings to other gods. So he provoked the Lord God of his fathers.

—2 Chronicles 28:25

And he turned again to build the high places that his father Hezekiah had torn down, and he set up altars to the Baals, and made Asherah poles, and worshiped the starry assembly of heaven and served them.

—2 Chronicles 33:3

Break the arm of the wicked and the evil ones; seek out their wickedness until You find none.

—Psalm 10:15

You will hide them in the secret of Your presence from conspirators; You will keep them secretly in a shelter from the strife of tongues.

—Psalm 31:20

Hide me from the secret counsel of the wicked, from the throng of workers of iniquity, who sharpen their tongue like a sword, and bend their bows to shoot their arrows—bitter words, that they may shoot in secret at the person of integrity; suddenly they shoot at him and do not fear.

—PSALM 64:2–4

A fire broke out among their company; the flame burned up the wicked.

—PSALM 106:18

Therefore He said that He would destroy them, had not Moses, His chosen one, stood before Him to intercede, to turn away His wrath from destroying them.

—PSALM 106:23

Let them curse, but You will bless; when they arise, let them be ashamed, but let Your servant rejoice.

—PSALM 109:28

The word of the LORD came to me the second time, saying, "What do you see?" And I said, "I see a boiling pot. And it is facing away from the north." Then the LORD said to me, "Out of the north an evil will break forth upon all the inhabitants of the land."

—JEREMIAH 1:13–14

They have built also the high places of Baal to burn their sons with fire for burnt offerings to Baal, which I did not command, nor speak, nor did it come into My mind.

—JEREMIAH 19:5

Therefore thus says the Lord GOD, "Your slain whom you have laid in the midst of it, they are the flesh and this city is the cauldron. But I will bring you forth out of the midst of it."

—EZEKIEL 11:7

The sword shall come upon Egypt, and great pain shall be in Ethiopia. When the slain fall in Egypt, they take away her wealth, and her foundations are broken down.

—EZEKIEL 30:4

When he shall stand up, his kingdom shall be broken and shall be divided toward the four winds of heaven, but not to his posterity, nor according to his dominion which he ruled. For his kingdom shall be plucked up, even for others besides them.

—DANIEL 11:4

Then I will cut off the cities of your land, and I will overthrow your strongholds; then I will cut off sorceries from your hand, and you will no longer have fortune-tellers; then I will cut off your idols and your sacred stones from among you, and you will no longer bow down to the work of your hands; then I will root out your Asherah idols from among you, and I will annihilate your cities. And in anger and wrath I will take vengeance on the nations that have not listened.

—MICAH 5:11–15

These are the things you will do: Speak truth each to his neighbor, and make judgments in your gates that are for truth, and justice, and peace.

—Zechariah 8:16

But Elymas the sorcerer (which is his name by interpretation) opposed them, trying to divert the proconsul from the faith. Then Saul, who also is called Paul, filled with the Holy Spirit, stared at him and said, "You son of the devil, enemy of all righteousness, full of deceit and of all fraud, will you not cease perverting the right ways of the Lord? Now, look! The hand of the Lord is against you, and you shall be blind, not seeing the sun for a time." Immediately mist and darkness fell on him, and he went about seeking someone to lead him by the hand.

—Acts 13:8–11

Many who believed came confessing and telling their deeds. Many who practiced magic brought their books together and burned them before everyone. They calculated their value, which equaled fifty thousand drachmas. So the word of the Lord powerfully grew and spread.

—Acts 19:18–20

O foolish Galatians! Who has bewitched you that you should not obey the truth? Before your eyes Jesus Christ was clearly portrayed among you as crucified.

—Galatians 3:1

Now the works of the flesh are revealed, which are these: adultery, sexual immorality, impurity, lewdness, idolatry, sorcery, hatred, strife, jealousy, rage, selfishness, dissensions, heresies, envy, murders, drunkenness, carousing, and the like. I warn you, as I previously warned you, that those who do such things shall not inherit the kingdom of God.

—GALATIANS 5:19–21

"Any victory that does not more than conquer is just an imitation victory. While we are suppressing and wrestling, we are only imitating victory. If Christ lives in us, we will rejoice in everything, and we will thank and praise the Lord. We will say, 'Hallelujah! Praise the Lord' forever."

WATCHMAN NEE

Chapter 4

BREAKING FREE FROM...

LUST AND PERVERSION

Then the men said to Lot, "Have you anyone else here? Sons-in-law, sons, daughters, or anyone you have in the city, take them out of this place! For we are about to destroy this place, because the outcry against its people has grown great before the presence of the LORD, and the LORD has sent us to destroy it."

—GENESIS 19:12–13

Then the LORD rained brimstone and fire on Sodom and Gomorrah. It was from the LORD out of heaven.

—GENESIS 19:24

I lay down and slept; I awoke, for the LORD sustained me.

—PSALM 3:5

Who can understand his errors? Cleanse me from secret faults.

—PSALM 19:12

Teach me Your way, O LORD, and lead me in an upright path, because of my enemies.

—PSALM 27:11

Teach me to do Your will, for You are my God; may Your good spirit lead me onto level ground.

—PSALM 143:10

Keep your heart with all diligence, for out of it are the issues of life. Put away from you a deceitful mouth, and put perverse lips far from you. Let your eyes look right on, and let your eyelids look straight before you.

—PROVERBS 4:23–25

I will bring the blind by a way that they did not know. I will lead them in paths that they have not known. I will make darkness light before them and crooked things straight. These things I will do for them and not forsake them.

—ISAIAH 42:16

They shall be turned back, they shall be greatly ashamed, who trust in graven images, who say to the molten images, "You are our gods."

—ISAIAH 42:17

Since you were precious in My sight, you have been honorable, and I have loved you. Therefore, I will give men for you, and people for your life. Do not fear, for I am with you. I will bring your descendants from the east, and gather you from the west.

—ISAIAH 43:4–5

And the LORD shall guide you continually, and satisfy your soul in drought, and strengthen your bones. And you shall be like a watered garden, and like a spring of water, whose waters do not fail.

—ISAIAH 58:11

I will greatly rejoice in the Lord, my soul shall be joyful in my God. For He has clothed me with the garments of salvation. He has covered me with the robe of righteousness, as a bridegroom decks himself with ornaments, and as a bride adorns herself with her jewels.

—Isaiah 61:10

Who is the wise man who may understand this? And who is he to whom the mouth of the Lord has spoken, that he may declare it? Why is the land ruined and burned up like a wilderness, so that no one passes through? And the Lord said, "Because they have forsaken My law which I set before them, and have not obeyed My voice, nor walked in it, but have walked after the imagination of their own heart and after the Baals, which their fathers taught them."

—Jeremiah 9:12–14

Those of you who escape shall remember Me among the nations wherever they shall be carried captives, because I am broken by their whorish heart which has departed from Me, and with their eyes which play the harlot after their idols. And they shall loathe themselves for the evils which they have committed in all their abominations.

—Ezekiel 6:9

My people seek counsel from their wood, and their staff informs them. For the spirit of harlotry has led them astray, and they have played the whore in defiance of their God.

—Hosea 4:12

And it will be on that day that I will set Jerusalem as a weighty stone to all the peoples. All who carry it will surely gash themselves, and all the nations of the land will be gathered against it.

—Zechariah 12:3

Did He not make them one, having a remnant of the Spirit? And why one? He seeks godly offspring. So take heed to your spirit, that you do not deal treacherously.

—Malachi 2:15

And lead us not into temptation, but deliver us from evil. For Yours is the kingdom, and the power, and the glory, forever. Amen.

—Matthew 6:13

So they brought the boy to Him. When He saw him, immediately the spirit dashed him, and he fell on the ground and wallowed, foaming at the mouth.

—Mark 9:20

But He turned and rebuked them and said, "You do not know what kind of spirit you are of. For the Son of Man did not come to destroy men's lives but to save them." And they went to another village.

—Luke 9:55–56

That you may be blameless and harmless, sons of God, without fault, in the midst of a crooked and perverse generation, in which you shine as lights in the world.

—Philippians 2:15

To the pure, all things are pure. But to those who are defiled and unbelieving, nothing is pure. Even their minds and consciences are defiled.

—Titus 1:15

But the wisdom that is from above is first pure, then peaceable, gentle, open to reason, full of mercy and good fruits, without partiality, and without hypocrisy. And the fruit of righteousness is sown in peace by those who make peace.

—James 3:17–18

For all that is in the world—the lust of the flesh, the lust of the eyes, and the pride of life—is not of the Father, but is of the world.

—1 John 2:16

But I have a few things against you: You permit that woman Jezebel, who calls herself a prophetess, to teach and seduce My servants to commit sexual immorality and eat food sacrificed to idols.

—Revelation 2:20

SEXUAL SIN

I urge you therefore, brothers, by the mercies of God, that you present your bodies as a living sacrifice, holy, and acceptable to God, which is your reasonable service of worship. Do not be conformed to this world, but be transformed by the renewing of your mind, that you may prove what is the good and acceptable and perfect will of God.

—ROMANS 12:1–2

Therefore put to death the parts of your earthly nature: sexual immorality, uncleanness, inordinate affection, evil desire, and covetousness, which is idolatry.

—COLOSSIANS 3:5

Do not be unequally yoked together with unbelievers. For what fellowship has righteousness with unrighteousness? What communion has light with darkness?

—2 CORINTHIANS 6:14

For this is the will of God, your sanctification: that you should abstain from sexual immorality, that each one of you should know how to possess his own vessel in sanctification and honor, not in the lust of depravity, even as the Gentiles who do not know God, and that no man take advantage of and defraud his brother in any matter, because the Lord is the avenger in all these things, as we also have forewarned you and testified. For God has not called us to uncleanness, but to holiness.

—1 THESSALONIANS 4:3–7

MORAL IMPURITY

And you shall love the LORD your God, with all your heart and with all your soul and with all your might. These words, which I am commanding you today, shall be in your heart.

You shall teach them diligently to your children and shall talk of them when you sit in your house, and when you walk by the way and when you lie down and when you rise up. You shall bind them as a sign on your hand, and they shall be as frontlets between your eyes. You shall write them on the doorposts of your house and on your gates.

—Deuteronomy 6:5–9

They have acted corruptly to Him. They are not His children, but blemished. They are a perverse and crooked generation. Is this how you repay the Lord, you foolish and unwise people? Is He not your father who has bought you? Has He not made you, and established you? Remember the days of old. Consider the years of previous generations. Ask your father, and he will show you, your elders, and they will tell you.

—Deuteronomy 32:5–7

In pride the wicked one is in hot pursuit of the poor. May they be caught in the devices they have planned.

—Psalm 10:2

Break the arm of the wicked and the evil ones; seek out their wickedness until You find none. The Lord is King forever and ever; the nations perished from His land.

—Psalm 10:15–16

I will set no wicked thing before my eyes. I hate the work of those who turn aside; it shall not have part of me. A perverted heart shall be far from me; I will not know anything wicked.

—Psalm 101:3–4

Why do you all scheme against the Lord? He will bring it to an end. It will not rise up a second time. Because they are like interwoven thorns and as drunkards imbibing, they are consumed like completely dry stubble.

—Nahum 1:9–10

But Jesus said, "Let the little children come to Me, and do not forbid them. For to such belongs the kingdom of heaven."

—Matthew 19:14

Those who are Christ's have crucified the flesh with its passions and lusts. If we live in the Spirit, let us also walk in the Spirit.

—Galatians 5:24–25

Who know the righteous requirement of God, that those who commit such things are worthy of death. They not only do them, but also give hearty approval to those who practice them.

—Romans 1:32

Unrepentance

Godly sorrow produces repentance that leads to salvation and brings no regret, but the sorrow of the world produces death.

—2 Corinthians 7:10

But we know that the judgment of God is according to truth against those who commit such things. Do you think, O man, who judges those who do such things, and who does the same thing, that you will escape the judgment of God? Do you despise the riches of His goodness, tolerance, and patience, not knowing that the goodness of God leads you to repentance?

—Romans 2:2–4

Pray for us. For we trust that we have a good conscience and in all things are willing to live honestly.

—Hebrews 13:18

Now the goal of this command is love from a pure heart, and from a good conscience, and from sincere faith.

—1 Timothy 1:5

Then the Lord knows how to rescue the godly from trial, and to keep the unrighteous under punishment for the Day of Judgment.

—2 Peter 2:9

BONDAGE

Therefore say to the children of Israel, I am the LORD, and I will bring you out from under the burdens of the Egyptians, and I will rid you out of their bondage, and I will redeem you with a stretched out arm and with great judgments.

—EXODUS 6:6

O sing to the LORD a new song, for He has done marvelous deeds! His right hand and His holy arm have accomplished deliverance.

—PSALM 98:1

Awake, awake, put on strength, O arm of the LORD. Awake as in the ancient days, in the generations of old. Was it not You who cut Rahab to pieces and wounded the dragon?

—ISAIAH 51:9

His brightness was like the light; rays flashed from His hand, and there His power was hidden.

—HABAKKUK 3:4

Escape from sexual immorality. Every sin that a man commits is outside the body. But he who commits sexual immorality sins against his own body.

—1 CORINTHIANS 6:18

A BROKEN HEART

Then He said, "I will make all My goodness pass before you, and I will proclaim the name of the LORD before you. I will be gracious to whom I will be gracious and will show mercy on whom I will show mercy."

—Exodus 33:19

The Lord is near to the brokenhearted, and saves the contrite of spirit.

—Psalm 34:18

He has put a new song in my mouth, even praise to our God; many will see it, and fear, and will trust in the Lord.

—Psalm 40:3

I will praise the name of God with a song, and will magnify Him with thanksgiving.

—Psalm 69:30

But You, O Lord, are a God full of compassion and gracious, slow to anger, and abundant in mercy and truth.

—Psalm 86:15

While I live I will praise the Lord; I will sing praises unto my God while I have my life. Do not put your trust in princes, nor in a person, in whom there is no deliverance.

—Psalm 146:2–3

He heals the broken in heart, and binds up their wounds.

—Psalm 147:3

Moreover the light of the moon shall be as the light of the sun, and the light of the sun shall be sevenfold, as the light of seven days, in the day that the LORD binds up the breach of His people and heals the wound from His blow.

—ISAIAH 30:26

Sing, O heavens! And be joyful, O earth! And break forth into singing, O mountains! For the LORD has comforted His people and will have mercy on His afflicted.

—ISAIAH 49:13

Indeed the LORD shall comfort Zion. He will comfort all her waste places. And He will make her wilderness like Eden and her desert like the garden of the LORD. Joy and gladness shall be found in it, thanksgiving, and the voice of melody.

—ISAIAH 51:3

EVIL

May the adversaries of my life be ashamed and confused; may those who seek my harm be enveloped in scorn and dishonor.

—PSALM 71:13

Surely the righteous man shall not be moved; the righteous shall be in everlasting remembrance. He shall not be afraid of evil tidings; his heart is fixed, trusting in the LORD. His heart is established; he shall not be afraid, until he sees triumph upon his enemies.

—PSALM 112:6–8

The LORD shall protect you from all evil; He shall preserve your soul. The LORD shall preserve your going out and your coming in from now and for evermore.

—PSALM 121:7–8

The LORD said, "Truly I will set you free for good purposes. Truly I will cause the enemy to entreat you in the time of evil and in the time of affliction."

—JEREMIAH 15:11

You went forth to deliver Your people, to deliver Your anointed one.

—HABAKKUK 3:13

I do not pray that You should take them out of the world, but that You should keep them from the evil one.

—JOHN 17:15

EMOTIONAL NEEDS

O God, do not be far from me; O my God, act quickly to help me.

—PSALM 71:12

I will pray the Father, and He will give you another Counselor, that He may be with you forever: The Spirit of truth, whom the world cannot receive, for it does not see Him, neither does it know Him. But you know Him, for He lives with you, and will be in you.

—JOHN 14:16–17

Godly sorrow produces repentance that leads to salvation and brings no regret, but the sorrow of the world produces death.

—2 Corinthians 7:10

Let your lives be without love of money, and be content with the things you have. For He has said, "I will never leave you, nor forsake you."

—Hebrews 13:5

For whatever was previously written was written for our instruction, so that through perseverance and encouragement of the Scriptures we might have hope.

—Romans 15:4

Financial Stress

But a mist arose from the earth and watered the whole surface of the ground.

—Genesis 2:6

Abraham called the name of that place The Lord Will Provide, as it is said to this day, "In the mount of the Lord it will be provided."

—Genesis 22:14

May those who favor my righteous cause shout for joy and be glad, may they say continually, "The Lord be magnified, who delights in the peace of His servant."

—Psalm 35:27

Praise the LORD! Blessed is the man who fears the LORD, who delights greatly in His commandments. His offspring shall be mighty in the land; the generation of the upright shall be blessed. Wealth and riches shall be in his house; and his righteousness endures forever.

—PSALM 112:1–3

Peace be within your walls and security within your towers.

—PSALM 122:7

That our granaries may be full, providing all manner of produce, that our sheep may bring forth thousands and ten thousands in our fields, that our oxen may be strong in labor, that there be no invaders breaking in nor captives going out, that there be no distress in our streets.

—PSALM 144:13–14

So your barns will be filled with plenty, and your presses will burst out with new wine.

—PROVERBS 3:10

Riches and honor are with me, yes, enduring riches and righteousness.

—PROVERBS 8:18

That I may cause those who love me to inherit wealth, and I will fill their treasuries.

—PROVERBS 8:21

A good man leaves an inheritance to his children's children, and the wealth of the sinner is laid up for the just.

—PROVERBS 13:22

I, even I, have spoken. Indeed, I have called him. I have brought him, and his way will prosper.

—ISAIAH 48:15

Thus says the LORD, your Redeemer, the Holy One of Israel. "I am the LORD your God who teaches you to profit, who leads you by the way that you should go."

—ISAIAH 48:17

I will make them and the places round about My hill a blessing. And I will cause the showers to come down in their season. They shall be showers of blessing.

—EZEKIEL 34:26

Then the threshing floors will be filled with grain, and the vats will overflow with new wine and oil.

—JOEL 2:24

"Indeed, the days are coming," says the LORD, "when the ploughman will overtake the one who is reaping, and the treader of grapes the one who is sowing the seed. The mountains will drip sweet wine, and all the hills will flow with it."

—AMOS 9:13

Give, and it will be given to you: Good measure, pressed down, shaken together, and running over, will men give unto you. For with the measure you use, it will be measured unto you.

—Luke 6:38

God is able to make all grace abound toward you, so that you, always having enough of everything, may abound to every good work.

—2 Corinthians 9:8

For you know the grace of our Lord Jesus Christ, that though He was rich, yet for your sakes He became poor, that through His poverty you might be rich.

—2 Corinthians 8:9

But when you cross the Jordan, and dwell in the land which the Lord your God has given you to inherit, and when He gives you rest from all your enemies round about, so that you dwell in safety, then there will be a place which the Lord your God will choose to cause His name to dwell. There you must bring all that I command you: your burnt offerings, and your sacrifices, your tithes, the offering of your hand, and all your choice vows which you vow to the Lord.

—Deuteronomy 12:10–11

Blessed be the Lord who has given rest to His people Israel according to all that He promised. Not one word of His promises which He gave by the hand of Moses His servant has failed.

—1 Kings 8:56

Come to Me, all you who labor and are heavily burdened, and I will give you rest.

—MATTHEW 11:28

WORRY ABOUT THE FUTURE

Do not fear, for I am with you. Do not be dismayed, for I am your God. I will strengthen you. Indeed, I will help you. Indeed, I will uphold you with My righteous right hand.

—ISAIAH 41:10

"For I know the plans that I have for you," says the LORD, "plans for peace and not for evil, to give you a future and a hope."

—JEREMIAH 29:11

"There is hope for your future," says the LORD, "that your children will come back to their own border."

—JEREMIAH 31:17

Then it will be that in the latter days, the mountain of the house of the LORD will be established as head of the mountains, and will be lifted up above the hills, and people will stream to it. And many nations will come and say, "Come, that we might go up to the mountain of the LORD and to the house of the God of Jacob, that He might teach us His ways and that we might walk in His paths." For from Zion will go forth the law, and the word of the LORD from Jerusalem.

—MICAH 4:1–2

Therefore we were buried with Him by baptism into death, that just as Christ was raised up from the dead by the glory of the Father, even so, we also should walk in newness of life. For if we have been united with Him in the likeness of His death, so shall we also be united with Him in the likeness of His resurrection.

—ROMANS 6:4–5

God is able to make all grace abound toward you, so that you, always having enough of everything, may abound to every good work.

—2 CORINTHIANS 9:8

And He raised us up and seated us together in the heavenly places in Christ Jesus. So that in the coming ages He might show the surpassing riches of His grace in kindness toward us in Christ Jesus. For by grace you have been saved through faith, and this is not of yourselves. It is the gift of God.

—EPHESIANS 2:6–8

For if by one man's trespass death reigned through him, then how much more will those who receive abundance of grace and the gift of righteousness reign in life through the One, Jesus Christ.

—ROMANS 5:17

But my God shall supply your every need according to His riches in glory by Christ Jesus.

—PHILIPPIANS 4:19

For every wild animal of the forest is mine, and the cattle on a thousand hills. I know every bird of the mountains, and the creatures that move in the field are mine. If I were hungry, I would not tell you; for the world is Mine, and all its fullness.

—Psalm 50:10–12

Light goes out for the righteous, and gladness for the upright in heart.

—Psalm 97:11

He satisfies your mouth with good things, so that your youth is renewed like the eagle's.

—Psalm 103:5

Therefore, the redeemed of the Lord shall return and come with singing to Zion. And everlasting joy shall be upon their head. They shall obtain gladness and joy. And sorrow and mourning shall flee away.

—Isaiah 51:11

The Lord your God is in your midst, a Mighty One, who will save. He will rejoice over you with gladness; He will quiet you with His love; He will rejoice over you with singing.

—Zephaniah 3:17

Therefore, I say to you, take no thought about your life, what you will eat, or what you will drink, nor about your body, what you will put on. Is not life more than food and the body than clothing? Look at the birds of the air, for they do not sow, nor do they reap, nor gather into barns. Yet your heavenly Father feeds them. Are you not much better than they?

—Matthew 6:25–26

Fear and Protection

Be strong and of a good courage. Fear not, nor be afraid of them, for the Lord your God, it is He who goes with you. He will not fail you, nor forsake you.

—Deuteronomy 31:6

It shall come to pass in the day that the Lord shall give you rest from your sorrow, and from your fear, and from the hard bondage in which you were made to serve.

—Isaiah 14:3

He shall be the stability of your times, a wealth of salvation, wisdom, and knowledge. The fear of the Lord is His treasure.

—Isaiah 33:6

Do not be afraid of sudden terror, nor of trouble from the wicked when it comes. For the Lord will be your confidence, and will keep your foot from being caught.

—Proverbs 3:25–26

That we should be saved from our enemies and from the hand of all who hate us.

—Luke 1:71

There is no fear in love, but perfect love casts out fear, because fear has to do with punishment. Whoever fears is not perfect in love.

—1 John 4:18

The angel of the Lord camps around those who fear Him, and delivers them.

—Psalm 34:7

Lead me out of the net that they have hidden for me, for You are my strength. Into Your hand I commit my spirit; You have redeemed me, O Lord, God of truth.

—Psalm 31:4–5

Deliver me from my enemies, O my God; give me refuge from those who rise up against me.

—Psalm 59:1

He led them in safety, so that they were not afraid, but the sea overwhelmed their enemies.

—Psalm 78:53

You are my hiding place and my shield, I hope in Your word.

—Psalm 119:114

Hold me up, and I shall be safe, and I will have respect for Your statutes continually.

—Psalm 119:117

WEAKNESS

And He said, "My presence will go with you, and I will give you rest."

—Exodus 33:14

The Lord is my strength and my shield; my heart trusted in Him, and I was helped; therefore my heart rejoices, and with my song I will thank Him.

—Psalm 28:7

Cast your care on the Lord, and He will sustain you; He will not allow the righteous to totter forever.

—Psalm 55:22

Unless the Lord had been my help, my soul would have lived in the land of silent death.

—Psalm 94:17

I will lift up my eyes to the hills, from where comes my help? My help comes from the Lord, who made heaven and earth. He will not let your foot slip; He who keeps you will not slumber.

—Psalm 121:1–3

Certainly God is my salvation. I will trust and not be afraid. For the Lord God is my strength and my song. He also has become my salvation.

—Isaiah 12:2

Trust in the LORD forever, for in GOD the LORD we have an everlasting rock.

—ISAIAH 26:4

But those who wait upon the LORD shall renew their strength. They shall mount up with wings as eagles. They shall run, and not be weary. And they shall walk, and not faint.

—ISAIAH 40:31

For the Lord GOD will help Me. Therefore, I shall not be disgraced. Therefore, I have set My face like a flint, and I know that I shall not be ashamed.

—ISAIAH 50:7

He satisfies your mouth with good things, so that your youth is renewed like the eagle's.

—PSALM 103:5

O LORD, my strength and my fortress, and my refuge in the day of affliction, the nations will come to You from the remote parts of the earth, and will say, "Surely our fathers have inherited lies, vanity, and things in which there is no profit."

—JEREMIAH 16:19

Their Redeemer is strong; the LORD of Hosts is His name. He will thoroughly plead their case, that He may give rest to the land, but disquiet to the inhabitants of Babylon.

—JEREMIAH 50:34

Teaching them to observe all things I have commanded you. And remember, I am with you always, even to the end of the age.

—Matthew 28:20

For this reason we do not lose heart: Even though our outward man is perishing, yet our inward man is being renewed day by day. Our light affliction, which lasts but for a moment, works for us a far more exceeding and eternal weight of glory, while we do not look at the things which are seen, but at the things which are not seen. For the things which are seen are temporal, but the things which are not seen are eternal.

—2 Corinthians 4:16–18

So I take pleasure in weaknesses, in reproaches, in hardships, in persecutions, and in distresses for Christ's sake. For when I am weak, then I am strong. I have become a fool in boasting. You have compelled me, for I ought to have been commended by you, for I am in no way inferior to the leading apostles, though I am nothing. Truly the signs of an apostle were performed among you in all patience, in signs and wonders, and mighty deeds.

—2 Corinthians 12:10–12

So we may boldly say, "The Lord is my helper, I will not fear. What can man do to me?"

—Hebrews 13:6

TEARS AND SORROW

And Hannah answered and said, "No, my lord, I am a woman of sorrow. I have drunk neither wine nor strong drink, but have poured out my soul before the LORD."

—1 SAMUEL 1:15

Arise, O LORD! O God, lift up Your hand! Do not forget the humble.

—PSALM 10:12

This poor man cried, and the LORD heard, and saved him out of all his troubles.

—PSALM 34:6

A righteous one keeps all his bones; not one of them is broken.

—PSALM 34:20

He restores my soul; He guides me in paths of righteousness for His name's sake.

—PSALM 23:3

Lord, all my desire is before You, and my sighing is not hidden from You. My heart throbs, my strength fails me; as for the light of my eyes, it also is gone from me.

—PSALM 38:9–10

Why are you cast down, O my soul? And why are you disquieted in me? Hope in God, for I will yet thank Him for the help of His presence.

—PSALM 42:5

You take account of my wandering; put my tears in Your bottle; are they not in Your book?

—Psalm 56:8

Those who sow in tears shall reap in joy.

—Psalm 126:5

He will swallow up death for all time, and the Lord God will wipe away tears from all faces. And the reproach of His people He shall take away from all the earth, for the Lord has spoken it.

—Isaiah 25:8

Go, and say to Hezekiah, "Thus says the Lord, the God of David your father, 'I have heard your prayer, I have seen your tears. Surely I will add to your days fifteen years.'"

—Isaiah 38:5

Your sun shall no more go down, nor shall your moon wane. For the Lord shall be your everlasting light, and the days of your mourning shall end.

—Isaiah 60:20

Then he said to them, "Go your way. Eat the fat, drink the sweet drink, and send portions to those for whom nothing is prepared; for this day is holy to our Lord. Do not be grieved, for the joy of the Lord is your strength."

—Nehemiah 8:10

Truly, truly I say to you that you will weep and lament, but the world will rejoice. You will be sorrowful, but your sorrow will be turned into joy. When a woman is giving birth, she has pain, because her hour has come. But as soon as she delivers the child, she no longer remembers the anguish for joy that a child is born into the world.

—John 16:20–21

Therefore guard your minds, be sober, and hope to the end for the grace that is to be brought to you at the revelation of Jesus Christ.

—1 Peter 1:13

"God shall wipe away all tears from their eyes. There shall be no more death." Neither shall there be any more sorrow nor crying nor pain, for the former things have passed away.

—Revelation 21:4

"The best way to keep the devil off our territory is to keep him busy on his own, defending his kingdom from our bold attacks.... Many of our battles are fought in view of heaven alone."

A. B. SIMPSON

Chapter 5

Battling With Authority

Battle With Authority

My son, let them not depart from your eyes—keep sound wisdom and discretion; so they will be life to your soul and grace to your neck. Then you will walk safely in your way, and your foot will not stumble.

—Proverbs 3:21–23

"For My thoughts are not your thoughts, and your ways are not My ways," says the Lord. "For as the heavens are higher than the earth, so are My ways higher than your ways and My thoughts higher than your thoughts."

—Isaiah 55:8–9

Now we have received not the spirit of the world, but the Spirit which is of God, so that we might know the things that are freely given to us by God.

—1 Corinthians 2:12

These things also we proclaim, not in the words which man's wisdom teaches, but which the Holy Spirit teaches, comparing spiritual things with spiritual. But the natural man does not receive the things of the Spirit of God, for they are foolishness to him; nor can he know them, because they are spiritually discerned.

—1 Corinthians 2:13–14

But He said to me, "My grace is sufficient for you, for My strength is made perfect in weakness." Therefore most gladly I will boast in my weaknesses, that the power of Christ may rest upon me.

—2 Corinthians 12:9

But when the Spirit of truth comes, He will guide you into all truth. For He will not speak on His own authority. But He will speak whatever He hears, and He will tell you things that are to come.

—John 16:13

So that the God of our Lord Jesus Christ, the Father of glory, may give you the Spirit of wisdom and revelation in the knowledge of Him. That the eyes of your heart may be enlightened, that you may know what is the hope of His calling and what are the riches of the glory of His inheritance among the saints.

—Ephesians 1:17–18

"This is the covenant that I will make with the house of Israel after those days," says the Lord: "I will put My laws into their minds and write them on their hearts, and I will be their God, and they shall be My people."

—Hebrews 8:10

For this reason He is the Mediator of a new covenant, since a death has occurred for the redemption of the sins that were committed under the first covenant, so that those who are called might receive the promise of eternal inheritance.

—Hebrews 9:15

As obedient children do not conduct yourselves according to the former lusts in your ignorance. But as He who has called you is holy, so be holy in all your conduct.

—1 Peter 1:14–15

Binding Demons of Fear

And he shall say to them, "Hear, O Israel, you approach today to do battle against your enemies. Do not be fainthearted. Do not fear, and do not tremble or be terrified because of them. For the Lord your God is He that goes with you, to fight for you against your enemies, to save you."

—Deuteronomy 20:3–4

For in the time of trouble He will hide me in His pavilion; in the shelter of His tabernacle He will hide me; He will set me up on a rock.

—Psalm 27:5

When the wicked came against me to eat my flesh—my enemies and my foes—they stumbled and fell. Though an army should encamp against me, my heart will not fear; though war should rise against me, in this will I be confident.

—Psalm 27:2–3

Heaviness in the heart of man makes it droop, but a good word makes it glad.

—Proverbs 12:25

In righteousness you shall be established. You shall be far from oppression, for you shall not fear, and from terror, for it shall not come near you.

—Isaiah 54:14

Be anxious for nothing, but in everything, by prayer and supplication with gratitude, make your requests known to God.

—Philippians 4:6

And the peace of God, which surpasses all understanding, will protect your hearts and minds through Christ Jesus.

—Philippians 4:7

For you have not received the spirit of slavery again to fear. But you have received the Spirit of adoption, by whom we cry, "Abba, Father."

—Romans 8:15

Whoever confesses that Jesus is the Son of God, God lives in him, and he in God. And we have come to know and to believe the love that God has for us. God is love. Whoever lives in love lives in God, and God in him. In this way, God's love is perfected in us, so that we may have boldness on the Day of Judgment, because as He is, so are we in this world.

—1 John 4:15–17

Cast all your care upon Him, because He cares for you.

—1 Peter 5:7

Binding the Enemy

Your right hand, O Lord, is glorious in power. Your right hand, O Lord, shatters the enemy. In the greatness of Your majesty, You throw down Your opponents. You unleash Your wrath; it consumes them like stubble.

—Exodus 15:6–7

He removed the high places, broke down the sacred pillars, cut down the Asherah poles, and crushed the bronze serpent that Moses had made, for until those days the Israelites had made offerings to it. They called it Nehushtan.

—2 Kings 18:4

"Because your heart was timid, and you humbled yourself before the Lord when you heard what I spoke against this place and against its inhabitants, that they should become a desolation and a curse, and you have torn your clothes and wept before Me, I also have heard you, declares the Lord. Therefore, I will gather you to your fathers, and you will be gathered to your grave in peace. Your eyes will not see all the evil which I am about to bring upon this place." Then they brought the king a report.

—2 Kings 22:19–20

He brought all the priests out of the cities of Judah and defiled the high places where the priests had made offerings, from Geba to Beersheba. He broke down the high places of the gates at the entry of the gates of Joshua the governor of the city, which were on the left at the gate of the city.

—2 Kings 23:8

He removed the pagan priests whom the kings of Judah had ordained to make offerings on the high places in the cities of Judah and the areas around Jerusalem. Those who made offerings to Baal, to the sun, the moon, and the constellations, that is, all the host of heaven.

—2 Kings 23:5

The king commanded all the people, "Keep the Passover to the Lord your God as it is written in this book of the covenant." For such a Passover had not been kept from the days of the judges who judged Israel, nor in all the days of the kings of Israel and the kings of Judah, but in the eighteenth year of King Josiah, this Passover was kept to the Lord in Jerusalem. Moreover Josiah disposed of the mediums, the soothsayers, the teraphim, the idols, and all the abominations that were seen in the land of Judah and in Jerusalem, so that he established the words of the law that were written in the book that Hilkiah the priest found in the house of the Lord.

—2 Kings 23:21–24

Can you draw out leviathan with a hook or snare his tongue with a line which you let down? Can you put a cord into his nose, or pierce his jaw with a hook?

—Job 41:1–2

Who has preceded Me that I should repay him? Everything under heaven is Mine.

—Job 41:11

You crushed the heads of Leviathan in pieces, and gave him for food to the people inhabiting the wilderness.

—Psalm 74:14

The Lord on high is mightier than the noise of many waters; yes, than the mighty waves of the sea.

—Psalm 93:4

Then they cried out to the Lord in their trouble, and He saved them out of their distress. He made the storm calm, and the sea waves were still.

—Psalm 107:28–29

In that day the Lord with His fierce and great and strong sword shall punish Leviathan the fleeing serpent, even Leviathan the twisted serpent. And He shall slay the dragon that is in the sea.

—Isaiah 27:1

Thus says the Lord, who makes a way in the sea and a path in the mighty waters.

—Isaiah 43:16

It is I who says to the deep, "Be dried up!" And I will dry up your rivers.

—Isaiah 44:27

Speak, and say, "Thus says the Lord God, 'I am against you, Pharaoh king of Egypt, the great dragon that lies in the midst of his rivers, which has said, "My Nile is my own, and I myself have made it."'"

—EZEKIEL 29:3

The ram which you saw having two horns represent the kings of Media and Persia.

—DANIEL 8:20

Then he said to me, "Do not be afraid, Daniel. For from the first day that you set your heart to understand this and to humble yourself before your God, your words were heard, and I have come because of your words. But the prince of the kingdom of Persia withstood me for twenty-one days. So Michael, one of the chief princes, came to help me, for I had been left there with the kings of Persia."

—DANIEL 10:12–13

I will give you the keys of the kingdom of heaven, and whatever you bind on earth shall be bound in heaven, and whatever you loose on earth shall be loosed in heaven.

—MATTHEW 16:19

Truly I say to you, whatever you bind on earth will be bound in heaven, and whatever you loose on earth will be loosed in heaven.

—MATTHEW 18:18

Immediately after the tribulation of those days, "the sun will be darkened, the moon will not give its light. The stars will fall from heaven, and the powers of the heavens will be shaken."

—Matthew 24:29

The seventy returned with joy, saying, "Lord, even the demons are subject to us through Your name." He said to them, "I saw Satan as lightning fall from heaven. Look, I give you authority to trample on serpents and scorpions, and over all the power of the enemy. And nothing shall by any means hurt you."

—Luke 10:17–19

To open their eyes and to turn them from darkness to light, and from the power of Satan to God, that they may receive forgiveness of sins and an inheritance among those who are sanctified by faith in Me.

—Acts 26:18

But now, having been freed from sin and having become slaves of God, you have fruit unto holiness, and the end is eternal life.

—Romans 6:22

Binding and Rejecting

Pharaoh's chariots and his army He has thrown into the sea. His chosen captains also are drowned in the Red Sea.

—Exodus 15:4

So I went in and saw every form of creeping things, and abominable beasts, and all the idols of the house of Israel, portrayed upon the wall round about.

—Ezekiel 8:10

Absalom acted this way toward every Israelite who came to the king for a judgment. So Absalom stole the hearts of the men of Israel.

—2 Samuel 15:6

He said to them, "Go and tell that fox, 'Look, I cast out demons. And I perform healings today and tomorrow, and on the third day I shall be perfected.'"

—Luke 13:32

Let no one deceive himself. If anyone among you seems to be wise in this world, let him become a fool that he may be wise.

—1 Corinthians 3:18

The great dragon was cast out, that ancient serpent called the Devil, or Satan, who deceives the whole world. He was cast down to the earth, and his angels were cast down with him.

—Revelation 12:9

BINDING WICKEDNESS IN HIGH PLACES

I will destroy your high places, and cut down your images, and cast your funeral offerings on the lifeless forms of your idols, and I shall abhor you.

—Leviticus 26:30

Then you will drive out all the inhabitants of the land from before you, and destroy all their carved images, and destroy all their molten images, and destroy all their high places.

—NUMBERS 33:52

"Because your heart was tender and you humbled yourself before God when you heard His words against this place and those who dwell here, and you have brought yourself low before Me and torn your clothes and wept before Me, I have heard you, declares the LORD. I am bringing you to be with your fathers, and you will be brought to your grave in peace, and your eyes will not see all the disaster that I am bringing on this place and on those who dwell here." So they returned this word to the king.

—2 CHRONICLES 34:27–28

Even if princes sit and conspire against me, Your servant will meditate on Your statutes. Your testimonies are my delight and my counselors.

—PSALM 119:23–24

The righteousness of the upright will direct his way, but the wicked will fall by his own wickedness. The righteousness of the upright will deliver them, but transgressors will be taken by their schemes.

—PROVERBS 11:5–6

But if I cast out demons by the Spirit of God, then the kingdom of God has come upon you.

—MATTHEW 12:28

The wrath of God is revealed from heaven against all ungodliness and unrighteousness of men, who suppress the truth through unrighteousness.

—Romans 1:18

In which you formerly walked according to the age of this world and according to the prince of the power of the air, the spirit who now works in the sons of disobedience.

—Ephesians 2:2

Put on the whole armor of God that you may be able to stand against the schemes of the devil. For our fight is not against flesh and blood, but against principalities, against powers, against the rulers of the darkness of this world, and against spiritual forces of evil in the heavenly places.

—Ephesians 6:11–12

As we await the blessed hope and the appearing of the glory of our great God and Savior Jesus Christ, who gave Himself for us, that He might redeem us from all lawlessness and purify for Himself a special people, zealous of good works.

—Titus 2:13–14

BURNING IDOLS

You shall have no other gods before Me.

—Exodus 20:3

He walked in all the ways that his father walked, served the idols that his father served, and worshipped them.

—2 Kings 21:21

If My people, who are called by My name, will humble themselves and pray, and seek My face and turn from their wicked ways, then I will hear from heaven, and will forgive their sin and will heal their land.

—2 Chronicles 7:14

Woe to the wicked! It shall be ill with him. For the reward of his hands shall be given him. As for My people, children are their oppressors, and women rule over them. O My people, those who lead you cause you to err, and destroy the way of your paths. The Lord stands up to plead and stands to judge the people. The Lord will enter into judgment with the elders and the princes of His people. "For you have eaten up the vineyard. The spoil of the poor is in your houses."

—Isaiah 3:11–14

And they will be as mighty men who trample down in the muddy streets in battle. They will fight because the Lord is with them, and He will put to shame those riding on horses.

—Zechariah 10:5

COMMANDING THE ENEMY TO LEAVE

For the holy ones who are in the land, they are the majestic ones; in them is all my delight.

—Psalm 16:3

The LORD frustrates the counsel of the nations; He restrains the purposes of the people. The counsel of the LORD stands forever, the purposes of His heart to all generations.

—PSALM 33:10–11

For the LORD of Hosts has purposed, and who shall disannul it? And His hand is stretched out, and who shall turn it back?

—ISAIAH 14:27

"Can the prey be taken from the mighty or the captives of a tyrant be delivered?" Indeed, thus says the LORD, "Even the captives of the mighty shall be taken away, and the prey of the tyrant shall be delivered. For I will contend with him who contends with you, and I will save your sons."

—ISAIAH 49:24–25

He called His twelve disciples to Him and gave them authority over unclean spirits, to cast them out, and to heal all kinds of sickness and all kinds of disease.

—MATTHEW 10:1

DEFEATING PRIDE AND REBELLION

They have now encircled us in our steps; they have set their eyes to bend down to the earth.

—PSALM 17:11

Blessed is the man who places trust in the LORD, but does not turn toward the proud, nor those falling away to falsehood.

—PSALM 40:4

Only by pride comes contention, but with the well-advised is wisdom.

—Proverbs 13:10

The Lord will destroy the house of the proud, but He will establish the border of the widow.

—Proverbs 15:25

Pride goes before destruction, and a haughty spirit before a fall.

—Proverbs 16:18

Take My yoke upon you, and learn from Me. For I am meek and lowly in heart, and you will find rest for your souls.

—Matthew 11:29

"But if you refuse and rebel, you shall be devoured with the sword." For the mouth of the Lord has spoken it.

—Isaiah 1:20

Out of them will proceed thanksgiving and the voice of those who make merry; and I will multiply them, and they will not be few. I will also glorify them, and they will not be small. Their children also will be as before, and their congregation will be established before Me; and I will punish all who oppress them.

—Jeremiah 30:19–20

Likewise you younger ones, submit yourselves to the elders. Yes, all of you be submissive one to another and clothe yourselves with humility, because "God resists the proud, and gives grace to the humble."

—1 Peter 5:5

With all humility, meekness, and patience, bearing with one another in love.

—Ephesians 4:2

Desert Places

Yet You in Your great mercy did not forsake them in the wilderness: The pillar of the cloud did not depart from them by day, to lead them in the way, nor the pillar of fire by night, to light for them the way they should go. You gave Your good Spirit to instruct them, did not withhold Your manna from their mouth, and gave them water for their thirst.

—Nehemiah 9:19–20

He split rocks in the wilderness and gave them abundance to drink as out of the great depths. He brought streams out of the rock and caused waters to run down like rivers.

—Psalm 78:15–16

He chose David His servant and took him from the sheepfolds. From following the nursing ewes He brought him to shepherd Jacob His people, and Israel His inheritance. So he shepherded them according to the integrity of his heart and guided them by the skillfulness of his hands.

—Psalm 78:70–72

But there the glorious Lord will be to us a place of broad rivers and streams on which no boat with oars shall go and on which no gallant ship shall pass.

—Isaiah 33:21

I will open rivers in high places, and fountains in the midst of the valleys. I will make the wilderness a pool of water, and the dry land springs of water. I will plant in the wilderness the cedar, the acacia, and the myrtle, and the olive tree. I will set in the desert the fir tree, and the pine, and the box tree together.

—Isaiah 41:18–19

You shall no more be termed, Forsaken, nor shall your land any more be termed, Desolate. But you shall be called, My Delight Is In Her, and your land, Married. For the Lord delights in you, and your land shall be married. For as a young man marries a virgin, so your sons shall marry you. And as the bridegroom rejoices over the bride, so your God shall rejoice over you.

—Isaiah 62:4–5

They will come with weeping, and with supplications I will lead them. I will cause them to walk by the rivers of waters, in a straight way in which they shall not stumble. For I am a father to Israel, and Ephraim is My firstborn.

—Jeremiah 31:9

Jesus said to her, "Everyone who drinks of this water will thirst again, but whoever drinks of the water that I shall give him will never thirst. Indeed, the water that I shall give him will become in him a well of water springing up into eternal life."

—John 4:13–14

He who believes in Me, as the Scripture has said, out of his heart shall flow rivers of living water.

—John 7:38

Divine Protection

Have You not made a hedge around him, around his household, and around all that he has on every side? You have blessed the work of his hands, and his possessions have increased in the land.

—Job 1:10

You are my hiding place; You will preserve me from trouble; You will surround me with shouts of deliverance.

—Psalm 32:7

As the mountains are around Jerusalem, so the Lord surrounds His people, from now and forever.

—Psalm 125:2

O God my Lord, the strength of my salvation, You have covered my head in the day of battle.

—Psalm 140:7

But the Lord stood with me and strengthened me, so that through me the preaching might be fully known, and that all the Gentiles might hear. And I was delivered out of the mouth of the lion.

—2 TIMOTHY 4:17

DOMINION OVER SIN

For their Redeemer is mighty; He will plead their cause with you.

—PROVERBS 23:11

I will feed those who oppress you with their own flesh. And they shall be drunk with their own blood as with sweet wine. And all flesh shall know that I the LORD am your Savior and your Redeemer, the Mighty One of Jacob.

—ISAIAH 49:26

Christ has redeemed us from the curse of the law by being made a curse for us—as it is written, "Cursed is every one who hangs on a tree."

—GALATIANS 3:13

To redeem those who were under the law, that we might receive the adoption as sons.

—GALATIANS 4:5

For sin shall not have dominion over you, for you are not under the law, but under grace.

—ROMANS 6:14

OPPRESSION

He will judge the world in righteousness, He will give judgment to the peoples in uprightness. The LORD also will be a refuge for the oppressed, a refuge in times of trouble. Those who know Your name will put their trust in You, for You, LORD, have not forsaken those who seek You.

—PSALM 9:8–10

From the wicked who bring ruin to me, from my deadly enemies who surround me.

—PSALM 17:9

For strangers rise up against me, and formidable adversaries seek my life; they do not set God before them.

—PSALM 54:3

Because of the voice of the enemy, because of the pressure of the wicked, for they cause trouble to drop on me, and in wrath they have animosity against me.

—PSALM 55:3

May he judge the poor of the people, may he save the children of the needy, and crush the oppressor.

—PSALM 72:4

Yet He raises up the poor from affliction and cares for their families like flocks of sheep. The righteous shall see it and rejoice, and all evil people shall stop their mouth. Whoever is wise let him observe these things; let them consider the lovingkindness of the Lord.

—Psalm 107:41–43

I have done what is right and just; do not abandon me to my oppressors. Be true to Your servant for good; let not the proud ones oppress me.

—Psalm 119:121–122

Who executes justice for the oppressed, who gives food to the hungry; the Lord releases the prisoners.

—Psalm 146:7

If you observe in a district an oppression of the poor and a robbing of justice and righteous, do not be astounded at this matter. For the high official is watched over by an even higher official, and there are even higher officials over them.

—Ecclesiastes 5:8

For oppression brings confusion to the wise person, and a bribe destroys a person's heart.

—Ecclesiastes 7:7

Let my outcasts dwell with you, Moab. Be a hiding place to them from the face of the destroyer. For the extortioner has come to an end. The destroyer ceases. The oppressors are consumed out of the land.

—Isaiah 16:4

Like a crane or a swallow, so I twitter. I mourn as a dove. My eyes look wistfully upward. O Lord, I am oppressed. Undertake for me.

—Isaiah 38:14

O house of David, thus says the Lord, "Execute justice each morning, and deliver him who has been robbed from the hand of the oppressor, lest My fury go out like fire and burn so that no one can quench it, because of the evil of your deeds."

—Jeremiah 21:12

I will seek that which was lost and bring back that which was driven away and bind up that which was broken and will strengthen that which was sick. But I will destroy the fat and the strong. I will feed them with judgment.

—Ezekiel 34:16

I will make with them a covenant of peace and will cause the wild beasts to cease from the land so that they dwell safely in the wilderness and sleep in the woods. I will make them and the places round about My hill a blessing. And I will cause the showers to come down in their season. They shall be showers of blessing.

—Ezekiel 34:25–26

Moreover the prince shall not take of the people's inheritance by oppression to thrust them out of their possession. But he shall give his sons inheritance out of his own possession so that My people not be scattered, every man from his possession.

—EZEKIEL 46:18

At that time I will deal with everyone who oppresses you; I will save the lame, and gather the outcast; I will give them praise and fame in every land where they have been put to shame.

—ZEPHANIAH 3:19

QUENCHING THE FIRE

Then he said to his servants, "See, Joab's field is next to mine, and he has barley there. Go, set it on fire." So the servants of Absalom set the field on fire.

—2 SAMUEL 14:30

An ungodly man digs up evil, and in his lips there is as a burning fire.

—PROVERBS 16:27

Where there is no wood, the fire goes out; so where there is no talebearer, the strife ceases.

—PROVERBS 26:20

And say to him, "Take heed, and be quiet. Do not fear nor be fainthearted because of the two tails of these smoking firebrands, because of the fierce anger of Rezin with Syria and of the son of Remaliah."

—ISAIAH 7:4

The burden of the beasts of the south. Through a land of trouble and anguish, from which comes the lioness and lion, the viper and fiery flying serpent, they will carry their riches on the shoulders of young donkeys, and their treasures on the humps of camels, to a people who shall not profit them.

—Isaiah 30:6

When you pass through the waters, I will be with you. And through the rivers, they shall not overflow you. When you walk through the fire, you shall not be burned. Neither shall the flame kindle on you.

—Isaiah 43:2

Before them fire devours and behind them a flame blazes. The land is like the Garden of Eden before them but behind them a desolate wasteland, and nothing escapes them.

—Joel 2:3

On that day I will set Judah like a fiery pot among wood and as a flaming torch among cut grain. And they will devour to the right and left all the surrounding peoples, while Jerusalem will still reside in her place, the place of Jerusalem.

—Zechariah 12:6

When Paul had gathered a bundle of sticks and put them on the fire, a viper driven out by the heat fastened on his hand.

—Acts 28:3

In order that the genuineness of your faith, which is more precious than gold that perishes, though it is tried by fire, may be found to result in praise, glory, and honor at the revelation of Jesus Christ.

—1 Peter 1:7

GOD'S SECURITY

Therefore You delivered them into the hand of their enemies, who afflicted them. When they cried to You in the time of their affliction, You heard from heaven, and, according to Your abundant mercy, You gave them deliverers who delivered them out of the hand of their enemies.

—Nehemiah 9:27

The Lord also will be a refuge for the oppressed, a refuge in times of trouble.

—Psalm 9:9

I have set the Lord always before me; because He is at my right hand, I will not be moved.

—Psalm 16:8

But the salvation of the righteous is from the Lord; He is their refuge in the time of distress.

—Psalm 37:39

And call on Me in the day of trouble; I will deliver you, and you will glorify Me.

—Psalm 50:15

He shall call upon Me, and I will answer him; I will be with him in trouble, and I will deliver him and honor him.

—Psalm 91:15

Unbelieving Spouse and a Healthy Marriage

So God created man in His own image, in the image of God He created him; male and female He created them.

—Genesis 1:27

Therefore a man will leave his father and his mother and be joined to his wife, and they will become one flesh. They were both naked, the man and his wife, and were not ashamed.

—Genesis 2:24–25

(For the Lord your God is a merciful God), He will not abandon you or destroy you or forget the covenant of your fathers which He swore to them.

—Deuteronomy 4:31

Those who know Your name will put their trust in You, for You, Lord, have not forsaken those who seek You.

—Psalm 9:10

I have been young, and now am old; yet I have not seen the righteous forsaken, nor their offspring begging bread.

—Psalm 37:25

If my father and my mother forsake me, then the LORD will take me in.

—PSALM 27:10

But as for me, I will walk in my integrity. Redeem me, and be gracious to me.

—PSALM 26:11

I will consider the path that is blameless. When will you come unto me? I will walk within my house with a perfect heart.

—PSALM 101:2

And I will give them one heart and one way, that they may fear Me forever, for their good and for their children after them.

—JEREMIAH 32:39

For your heavenly Father knows that you have need of all these things.

—MATTHEW 6:32

Now to the married I command, not I, but the Lord, do not let the wife depart from her husband. But if she departs, let her remain unmarried or be reconciled to her husband. And do not let the husband divorce his wife.

—1 CORINTHIANS 7:10–11

And if the woman has an unbelieving husband who consents to live with her, she should not divorce him. For the unbelieving husband is sanctified by the wife, and the unbelieving wife is sanctified by the husband. Otherwise, your children would be unclean. But now they are holy.

—1 Corinthians 7:13–14

But if the unbeliever departs, let that one depart. A brother or a sister is not bound in such cases. God has called us to peace. For how do you know, O wife, whether you will save your husband? Or how do you know, O husband, whether you will save your wife?

—1 Corinthians 7:15–16

"I will be a Father to you, and you shall be My sons and daughters," says the Lord Almighty.

—2 Corinthians 6:18

Likewise you wives, be submissive to your own husbands, so that if any do not obey the word, they may be won without a word by the conduct of their wives, as they see the purity and reverence of your lives.

—1 Peter 3:1–2

Likewise, you husbands, live considerately with your wives, giving honor to the woman as the weaker vessel, since they too are also heirs of the grace of life, so that your prayers will not be hindered.

—1 Peter 3:7

"But have we Holy Spirit power—power that restricts the devil's power, pulls down strongholds, and obtains promises? Daring delinquents will be damned if they are not delivered from the devil's dominion. What has hell to fear other than a God-anointed, prayer-powered church?"

LEONARD RAVENHILL

Chapter 6

WONDERS AND MIRACLES

HEALING

He said, "If you diligently listen to the voice of the LORD your God, and do what is right in His sight, and give ear to His commandments, and keep all His statutes, I will not afflict you with any of the diseases with which I have afflicted the Egyptians. For I am the LORD who heals you."

—EXODUS 15:26

O LORD my God, I cried to You, and You healed me. O LORD, You have brought up my soul from the grave; You have kept me alive, that I should not go down to the pit.

—PSALM 30:2–3

The LORD will sustain them on the sickbed; You will restore all his lying down in his illness.

—PSALM 41:3

With long life I will satisfy him and show him My salvation.

—PSALM 91:16

Who forgives all your iniquities, who heals all your diseases.

—PSALM 103:3

He sent His word and healed them and delivered them from their destruction.

—PSALM 107:20

I shall not die, but I shall live and declare the works of the LORD.

—PSALM 118:17

It will be health to your body, and strength to your bones.

—PROVERBS 3:8

He said, "Go, and tell this people, 'Listen indeed, but understand not, and see indeed, but perceive not.' Make the heart of this people fat, and make their ears heavy, and shut their eyes. Lest they see with their eyes, and hear with their ears, and understand with their hearts, and convert, and be healed."

—ISAIAH 6:9–10

It shall come to pass in that day that His burden shall be taken away from off your shoulder and His yoke from off your neck, and the yoke shall be destroyed because of the anointing oil.

—ISAIAH 10:27

So shall My word be that goes forth out of My mouth. It shall not return to Me void, but it shall accomplish that which I please, and it shall prosper in the thing for which I sent it.

—ISAIAH 55:11

Then you shall call, and the LORD shall answer. You shall cry, and He shall say, "Here I am."

—ISAIAH 58:9

I will bring it health and healing, and I will heal them; and I will reveal to them the abundance of peace and truth.

—Jeremiah 33:6

When the evening came, they brought to Him many who were possessed with demons. And He cast out the spirits with His word, and healed all who were sick.

—Matthew 8:16

Then a woman, who was ill with a flow of blood for twelve years, came behind Him and touched the hem of His garment.

—Matthew 9:20

And when the men of that place recognized Him, they sent word to all the surrounding country and brought to Him all who were sick, and begged Him that they might only touch the hem of His garment. And as many as touched it were made perfectly well.

—Matthew 14:35–36

He laid His hands on them and departed from there.

—Matthew 19:15

And whatever you ask in prayer, if you believe, you will receive.

—Matthew 21:22

For truly I say to you, whoever says to this mountain, "Be removed and be thrown into the sea," and does not doubt in his heart, but believes that what he says will come to pass, he will have whatever he says. Therefore I say to you, whatever

things you ask when you pray, believe that you w
them, and you will have them.

—MARK 11:23

Believers were increasingly added to the Lord, crowds of both
men and women, so that they even brought the sick out into
the streets and placed them on beds and mats, that at least
the shadow of Peter passing by might touch some of them.
Crowds also came out of the cities surrounding Jerusalem,
bringing the sick and those who were afflicted by evil spirits,
and they were all healed.

—ACTS 5:14–16

These signs will accompany those who believe: In My name
they will cast out demons; they will speak with new tongues.

—MARK 16:17

And He looked around to see her who had done it. But the
woman, fearing and trembling, knowing what had happened
to her, came and fell down before Him and told Him the
entire truth. He said to her, "Daughter, your faith has made
you well. Go in peace, and be healed of your affliction."

—MARK 5:32–34

When He was in a certain city, a man full of leprosy, upon
seeing Jesus, fell on his face and begged Him, "Lord, if You
will, You can make me clean." He reached out His hand and
touched him, saying, "I will. Be clean." And immediately the
leprosy left him.

—LUKE 5:12–13

ן who had a spirit of infirmity for
bent over and could not straighten
w her, He called her and said to her,
rom your infirmity." Then He laid
nmediately she was made straight

—LUKE 13:11–13

So handkerchiefs or aprons he had touched were brought to
the sick, and the diseases left them, and the evil spirits went
out of them.

—ACTS 19:12

It happened that the father of Publius lay sick with a fever
and dysentery. Paul visited him and, placing his hands on
him, prayed and healed him.

—ACTS 28:8

But now, having been freed from sin and having become
slaves of God, you have fruit unto holiness, and the end is
eternal life.

—ROMANS 6:22

Likewise, the Spirit helps us in our weaknesses, for we do not
know what to pray for as we ought, but the Spirit Himself
intercedes for us with groanings too deep for words.

—ROMANS 8:26

So that the blessing of Abraham might come on the Gentiles through Jesus Christ, that we might receive the promise of the Spirit through faith.

—GALATIANS 3:14

For we do not have a High Priest who cannot sympathize with our weaknesses, but One who was in every sense tempted like we are, yet without sin.

—HEBREWS 4:15

Is anyone sick among you? Let him call for the elders of the church, and let them pray over him, anointing him with oil in the name of the Lord. And the prayer of faith will save the sick, and the Lord will raise him up. And if he has committed any sins, he will be forgiven.

—JAMES 5:14–15

When you were buried with Him in baptism, in which also you are risen with Him through the faith of the power of God, who has raised Him from the dead. And you, being dead in your sins and the uncircumcision of your flesh, He has resurrected together with Him, having forgiven you all sins.

—COLOSSIANS 2:12–13

Through Him you believe in God who raised Him up from the dead and gave Him glory, so that your faith and hope might be in God.

—1 PETER 1:21

Overcoming Sickness and Infirmity

You shall serve the Lord your God, and He shall bless your bread and your water, and I will remove sickness from your midst.

—Exodus 23:25

His flesh will be fresher than a child's; he will return to the days of his youth.

—Job 33:25

A righteous one keeps all his bones; not one of them is broken.

—Psalm 34:20

The Lord is my light and my salvation; whom will I fear? The Lord is the strength of my life; of whom will I be afraid?

—Psalm 27:1

There shall be no evil befall you, neither shall any plague come near your tent.

—Psalm 91:10

The mountains melt like wax at the presence of the Lord, at the presence of the Lord of the earth.

—Psalm 97:5

Who forgives all your iniquities, who heals all your diseases.

—Psalm 103:3

He sent His word and healed them and delivered them from their destruction.

—Psalm 107:20

My soul collapses on account of grief; strengthen me according to Your word.

—Psalm 119:28

I will praise you, for You made me with fear and wonder; marvelous are Your works, and You know me completely.

—Psalm 139:14

For they are life to those who find them, and health to all their body.

—Proverbs 4:22

Until a dart struck through his liver. As a bird hastens to the snare, and knows not that it is for his life.

—Proverbs 7:23

A sound heart is the life of the flesh, but envy the rottenness of the bones.

—Proverbs 14:30

The light of the eyes rejoices the heart, and a good report makes the bones healthy.

—Proverbs 15:30

The wilderness and the solitary place shall be glad. And the desert shall rejoice and blossom as the rose.

—Isaiah 35:1

He said to me, "Son of man, can these bones live?" And I answered, "O Lord God, You know." Again He said to me,

"Prophesy over these bones and say to them, 'O dry bones, hear the word of the LORD.'"

—EZEKIEL 37:3–4

And it will be that in that day the mountains will drip sweet wine, and the hills will flow with milk, and all the streambeds of Judah will flow with water. A spring will proceed from the house of the LORD and will water the valley of Shittim.

—JOEL 3:18

But for you who fear My name, the Sun of Righteousness will rise with healing in His wings. You will go out and grow up like calves from the stall.

—MALACHI 4:2

Jesus went throughout all Galilee teaching in their synagogues, preaching the gospel of the kingdom, and healing all kinds of sickness and all sorts of diseases among the people.

—MATTHEW 4:23

To fulfill what was spoken by Isaiah the prophet, "He Himself took our infirmities and bore our sicknesses."

—MATTHEW 8:17

So He stood over her and rebuked the fever, and it left her. And immediately she rose and served them.

—LUKE 4:39

On a certain day, as He was teaching, Pharisees and teachers of the law were sitting nearby, who had come from every town

of Galilee and Judea and from Jerusalem. And the power of
the Lord was present to heal the sick.

—Luke 5:17

And they were all amazed at the mighty power of God.

—Luke 9:43

In the temple He found those who were selling oxen and
sheep and doves, and the moneychangers sitting there. When
He had made a whip of cords, He drove them all out of the
temple, with the sheep and oxen. He poured out the changers'
money and overturned the tables.

—John 2:14–15

Peter said to him, "Aeneas, Jesus the Christ heals you. Rise
up and make your bed." And immediately he rose up.

—Acts 9:34

What? Do you not know that your body is the temple of the
Holy Spirit, who is in you, whom you have received from
God, and that you are not your own? You were bought with
a price. Therefore glorify God in your body and in your spirit,
which are God's.

—1 Corinthians 6:19–20

By this we know that we are of the truth, and shall reassure
our hearts before Him. For if our heart condemns us, God is
greater than our heart and knows everything. Beloved, if our
heart does not condemn us, then we have confidence before
God.

—1 John 3:19–21

Beloved, I pray that all may go well with you and that you may be in good health, even as your soul is well. For I greatly rejoiced when brothers came and testified of the truth that is in you, just as you walk in the truth.

3 John 2–3

God's Presence in the Valleys

I thought it good to declare the signs and wonders that the Most High God has done for me. How great are His signs, and how mighty are His wonders! His kingdom is an everlasting kingdom, and His dominion is from generation to generation.

—Daniel 4:2–3

Even though I walk through the valley of the shadow of death, I will fear no evil for You are with me; Your rod and Your staff they comfort me. You prepare a table before me in the presence of my enemies; You anoint my head with oil; my cup runs over.

—Psalm 23:4–5

He turns a wilderness into pools of water, a parched ground into springs of water.

—Psalm 107:35

You visit the earth, and water it, You enrich it with the river of God, which is full of water; You prepare their grain, for thus You have established it. You water its furrows abundantly;

You settle its ridges; You soften it with showers; You bless its sprouting.

—Psalm 65:9–10

My son, attend to my words; incline your ear to my sayings. Do not let them depart from your eyes; keep them in the midst of your heart. For they are life to those who find them, and health to all their body.

—Proverbs 4:20–22

Pleasant words are as a honeycomb, sweet to the soul, and health to the bones.

—Proverbs 16:24

Strengthen the weak hands, and support the feeble knees. Say to those who are of a fearful heart, "Be strong, fear not. Your God will come with vengeance, even God with a recompense. He will come and save you."

—Isaiah 35:3–4

They shall not hunger nor thirst. Neither shall the heat nor sun strike them. For He who has mercy on them shall lead them, even by the springs of water He shall guide them. I will make all My mountains a road, and My highways shall be raised up.

—Isaiah 49:10–11

Therefore, I will allure her, and bring her into the wilderness, and speak tenderly to her. From there, I will give her vineyards to her, and the valley of Achor as a door of hope.

—Hosea 2:14–15

Blessed are those who hunger and thirst for righteousness, for they shall be filled.

—Matthew 5:6

Come to Me, all you who labor and are heavily burdened, and I will give you rest.

—Matthew 11:28

Every valley shall be filled, and every mountain and hill shall be brought low. And the crooked shall be made straight, and the rough ways shall be made smooth.

—Luke 3:5

But whoever drinks of the water that I shall give him will never thirst. Indeed, the water that I shall give him will become in him a well of water springing up into eternal life.

—John 4:14

And whoever calls on the name of the Lord shall be saved.

—Acts 2:21

For I know that through your prayer and the support of the Spirit of Jesus Christ, this will result in my deliverance.

—Philippians 1:19

Then he showed me a pure river of the water of life, clear as crystal, flowing from the throne of God and of the Lamb in the middle of its street. On each side of the river was the tree of life, which bore twelve kinds of fruit, yielding its fruit each month. The leaves of the tree were for the healing of the nations. There shall be no more curse. The throne of God and of the Lamb shall be in it, and His servants shall serve Him.

—Revelation 22:1–3

The Blood

For this is My blood of the new covenant, which is shed for many for the remission of sins.

—Matthew 26:28

When Jesus had stood up and saw no one but the woman, He said to her, "Woman, where are your accusers? Did no one condemn you?"

—John 8:10

And to reconcile all things to Himself by Him, having made peace through the blood of His cross, by Him, I say, whether they are things in earth, or things in heaven.

—Colossians 1:20

In Him we have redemption through His blood and the forgiveness of sins according to the riches of His grace.

—Ephesians 1:7

Therefore, brothers, we have confidence to enter the Most Holy Place by the blood of Jesus.

—Hebrews 10:19

Then He says, "Their sins and iniquities will I remember no more."

—Hebrews 10:17

You have not yet resisted to bloodshed while striving against sin.

—HEBREWS 12:4

And to Jesus, the Mediator of a new covenant; and to the sprinkled blood that speaks better than that of Abel.

—HEBREWS 12:24

Now may the God of peace, who through the blood of the eternal covenant brought again from the dead our Lord Jesus, the Great Shepherd of the sheep, make you perfect in every good work to do His will, working in you that which is pleasing in His sight, through Jesus Christ, to whom be glory forever and ever. Amen.

—HEBREWS 13:20–21

Then I heard a loud voice in heaven, saying, "Now the salvation and the power and the kingdom of our God and the authority of His Christ have come. For the accuser of our brothers, who accused them before our God day and night, has been cast down."

—REVELATION 12:10

They overcame him by the blood of the Lamb and by the word of their testimony. They loved not their lives unto the death. Therefore rejoice, you heavens and you who dwell in them! Woe unto the inhabitants of the earth and sea! For the devil has gone down to you with great wrath, because he knows that his time is short.

—REVELATION 12:11–12

THE TRINITY

The heavens declare the glory of God, and the firmament shows His handiwork.

—PSALM 19:1

For the LORD Most High is awesome; He is a great King over all the earth. He subdued peoples under us, and nations under our feet.

—PSALM 47:2–3

May his name endure forever; may his name increase as long as the sun; and may people bless themselves by him; may all nations call him blessed.

—PSALM 72:17

The LORD reigns; He is clothed with majesty; the LORD is robed with a belt of strength. Indeed, the world is established; it cannot be moved.

—PSALM 93:1

The LORD reigns; let the earth rejoice; let the many coastlands be glad!

—PSALM 97:1

The LORD has made known His salvation; His righteousness He has revealed in the sight of the nations. He has remembered His mercy and His faithfulness toward the house of Israel; all the ends of the earth have seen the deliverance of our God.

—PSALM 98:2–3

For I know that the LORD is great, and that our Lord is above all gods. Whatever the LORD pleases, He does in heaven and on earth, in the seas and all the depths. He causes the clouds to ascend from the ends of the earth; He makes lightning for the rain; he brings the wind out from His storehouses.

—PSALM 135:5–7

Your name, O LORD, endures forever; and Your renown, O LORD, throughout all generations. For the LORD will defend His people, and He will have compassion on His servants.

—PSALM 135:13–14

For unto us a child is born, unto us a son is given, and the government shall be upon his shoulder. And his name shall be called Wonderful Counselor, Mighty God, Eternal Father, Prince of Peace. Of the increase of his government and peace there shall be no end, upon the throne of David and over his kingdom, to order it and to establish it with justice and with righteousness, from now until forever. The zeal of the LORD of Hosts will perform this.

—ISAIAH 9:6–7

And he said, "This is the word of the LORD to Zerubbabel, saying, 'Not by might nor by power, but by My Spirit,' says the LORD of Hosts."

—ZECHARIAH 4:6

Whoever practices sin is of the devil, for the devil has been sinning from the beginning. For this purpose the Son of God was revealed, that He might destroy the works of the devil.

—1 JOHN 3:8

Then Peter said, "I have no silver and gold, but I give you what I have. In the name of Jesus Christ of Nazareth, rise up and walk."

—ACTS 3:6

Now, Lord, look on their threats and grant that Your servants may speak Your word with great boldness, by stretching out Your hand to heal and that signs and wonders may be performed in the name of Your holy Son Jesus.

—ACTS 4:29–30

I say then, walk in the Spirit, and you shall not fulfill the lust of the flesh. For the flesh lusts against the Spirit, and the Spirit against to the flesh. These are in opposition to one another, so that you may not do the things that you please.

—GALATIANS 5:16–17

Now may the God of hope fill you with all joy and peace in believing, so that you may abound in hope, through the power of the Holy Spirit.

—ROMANS 15:13

RELEASING GOD'S POWER

Your right hand, O Lord, is glorious in power. Your right hand, O Lord, shatters the enemy.

—Exodus 15:6

To You, O Lord, is the greatness, and the power, and the glory, and the victory, and the majesty, for everything in the heavens and the earth is Yours. Yours is the kingdom, O Lord, and You exalt Yourself as head above all.

—1 Chronicles 29:11

Riches and honor flow from You, and You rule over all. In Your hand are power and might, and in Your hand it is to make great and to strengthen all.

—1 Chronicles 29:12

For the word of the Lord is upright, and all His work is done in truth. He loves righteousness and justice; the earth is full of the lovingkindness of the Lord.

—Psalm 33:4–5

Gird Your sword on Your thigh, O Mighty One, with Your splendor and Your majesty. In Your majesty ride prosperously because of truth and meekness and righteousness; and Your right hand will teach You awesome things.

—Psalm 45:3–4

Deliver me from the workers of iniquity, and save me from bloodthirsty people. For they lie in wait for my life; the mighty are gathered against me, not for my transgression, nor for my sin, O LORD.

—PSALM 59:2–3

He rules by His power forever; His eyes keep watch on the nations; do not let the rebellious exalt themselves.

—PSALM 66:7

Blessed be His glorious name forever; and may the whole earth be filled with His glory. Amen, and Amen.

—PSALM 72:19

You have a mighty arm, and strong is Your hand, and victorious is Your right hand.

—PSALM 89:13

Who knows the power of Your anger? Or Your wrath according to Your fear?

—PSALM 90:11

He has shown His people the power of His works, that He may give them the inheritance of the nations. The works of His hands are true and just; all His commands are sure. They stand forever and ever, and are done in truth and uprightness.

—PSALM 111:6–8

Through Your precepts I receive understanding, therefore I hate every false way.

—PSALM 119:104

Let the high praises of God be in their mouths, and two-edged swords in their hands; to execute vengeance on the nations, and punishments on the peoples; to bind their kings with chains, and their nobles with shackles of iron; to execute upon them the written judgment; this is honor for all His godly ones. Praise the LORD!

—PSALM 149:6–9

O LORD, be gracious to us. We have waited for You. Be our strength every morning, our salvation also in the time of trouble.

—ISAIAH 33:2

See, the Lord GOD will come with a strong hand, and His arm shall rule for Him. See, His reward is with Him, and His recompense before Him. He shall feed His flock like a shepherd. He shall gather the lambs with His arm, and carry them in His bosom, and shall gently lead those that are with young.

—ISAIAH 40:10–11

"Is not My word like fire?" says the LORD, "and like a hammer that breaks the rock in pieces?"

—JEREMIAH 23:29

But seek first the kingdom of God and His righteousness, and all these things shall be given to you. Therefore, take no thought about tomorrow, for tomorrow will take thought about the things of itself. Sufficient to the day is the trouble thereof.

—MATTHEW 6:33–34

It is the Spirit who gives life. The flesh profits nothing. The words that I speak to you are spirit and are life.

—John 6:63

But you shall receive power when the Holy Spirit comes upon you. And you shall be My witnesses in Jerusalem, and in all Judea and Samaria, and to the ends of the earth.

—Acts 1:8

My speech and my preaching was not with enticing words of man's wisdom, but in demonstration of the Spirit and of power, so that your faith should not stand in the wisdom of men, but in the power of God.

—1 Corinthians 2:4–5

Now to Him who is able to do exceedingly abundantly beyond all that we ask or imagine, according to the power that works in us.

—Ephesians 3:20

For the Scripture says to Pharaoh, "For this very purpose I have raised you up, that I may show My power in you, and that My name may be proclaimed in all the earth."

—Romans 9:17

By the power of signs and wonders, by the power of the Spirit of God, so that from Jerusalem and as far around as Illyricum, I have fully preached the gospel of Christ.

—Romans 15:19

Let us labor therefore to enter that rest, lest anyone fall by the same pattern of unbelief. For the word of God is alive, and active, and sharper than any two-edged sword, piercing even to the division of soul and spirit, of joints and marrow, and able to judge the thoughts and intents of the heart.

—Hebrews 4:11–12

Whereas angels, who are greater in power and might, do not bring slanderous accusations against them before the Lord.

—2 Peter 2:11

Praying for the Nation

Do not defile yourselves in any of these ways, for in these practices the nations I am casting out before you have defiled themselves.

—Leviticus 18:24

The God of Israel said, the Rock of Israel spoke to me, "The one who rules over man justly, who rules in the fear of God."

—2 Samuel 23:3

Because if you return to the Lord, your brothers and children will find compassion before those who have taken them captive, in order to return you to this land. For the Lord your God is gracious and compassionate. He will not turn His face from you if you all return to Him.

—2 Chronicles 30:9

All the ends of the world will remember and turn to the LORD; and all the families of the nations will worship before You.

—PSALM 22:27

For they will quickly wither like the grass, and fade like the green herbs.

—PSALM 37:2

May God be gracious to us, and bless us, and cause His face to shine on us; Selah.

—PSALM 67:1

May all kings bow down before him; may all nations serve him.

—PSALM 72:11

Return again, O God of Hosts. Look down from heaven, and behold, have regard for this vine, and the root that Your right hand has planted, and the shoots that You made strong for Yourself.

—PSALM 80:14–15

All who serve graven images are ashamed, who boast in worthless idols; worship Him, all you gods.

—PSALM 97:7

O sing unto the LORD a new song; sing unto the LORD, all the earth! Sing unto the LORD, bless His name; declare His salvation from day to day. Proclaim His glory among the nations, His wonders among all peoples.

—Psalm 96:1–3

The Lord reigns; let the peoples tremble! He sits enthroned between the cherubim; let the earth shake.

—Psalm 99:1

Save us, we ask You, O Lord; O Lord, we ask You, send now success.

—Psalm 118:25

Turn away my eyes from beholding worthlessness, and revive me in Your way. Establish Your word to Your servant, so that You are feared. Turn away my reproach that I dread, for your judgments are good. Behold, I have a longing for Your precepts; revive me in Your righteousness.

—Psalm 119:37–40

The king's heart is in the hand of the Lord, as the rivers of water; He turns it to any place He will.

—Proverbs 21:1

But the wicked will be cut off from the earth, and the transgressors will be rooted out of it.

—Proverbs 2:22

The people who walked in darkness have seen a great light. Those who dwell in the land of the shadow of death, upon them the light has shined.

—Isaiah 9:2

See, a king shall reign in righteousness, and princes shall rule justly.

—Isaiah 32:1

Then the glory of the Lord shall be revealed, and all flesh shall see it together, for the mouth of the Lord has spoken it.

—Isaiah 40:5

For I will pour water on him who is thirsty, and floods on the dry ground. I will pour out My Spirit on your descendants, and My blessing on your offspring.

—Isaiah 44:3

Turn to Me and be saved, all the ends of the earth. For I am God, and there is no other.

—Isaiah 45:22

All your sons shall be taught of the Lord. And great shall be the peace of your sons.

—Isaiah 54:13

And I will give you shepherds according to My heart, who shall feed you with knowledge and understanding.

—Jeremiah 3:15

It shall come to pass that every living creature which moves to any place the rivers shall come, shall live. And there shall be a very great multitude of fish, because these waters shall come there and the others become healed. Thus everything shall live wherever the river comes.

—Ezekiel 47:9

For the earth will be filled with the knowledge of the glory of the LORD, as the waters cover the seas.

—HABAKKUK 2:14

And I will pour out on the house of David and over those dwelling in Jerusalem a spirit of favor and supplication so that they look to Me, whom they have pierced through. And they will mourn over Him as one mourns for an only child and weep bitterly over Him as a firstborn.

—ZECHARIAH 12:10

"If we would endeavor like brave men to stand in the battle, surely we should feel the assistance of God from Heaven. For He who giveth us occasion to fight, to the end that we may get the victory, is ready to succor those that fight and that trust in His grace."

THOMAS À KEMPIS

Chapter 7

KEYS TO THE KINGDOM

COVENANT PLAN

Let the peoples praise You, O God; let all the peoples praise You. Oh, let the nations be glad and sing for joy; for You will judge the people uprightly, and lead the nations on earth. Selah.

—PSALM 67:3–4

The wilderness and the solitary place shall be glad. And the desert shall rejoice and blossom as the rose. It shall blossom abundantly and rejoice even with joy and singing. The glory of Lebanon shall be given to it, the excellency of Carmel and Sharon. They shall see the glory of the LORD and the excellency of our God.

—ISAIAH 35:1–2

"For the mountains may be removed, and the hills may shake, but My kindness shall not depart from you, nor shall My covenant of peace be removed," says the LORD who has mercy on you.

—ISAIAH 54:10

To proclaim the acceptable year of the LORD and the day of vengeance of our God; to comfort all who mourn, to preserve those who mourn in Zion, to give to them beauty for ashes, the oil of joy for mourning, the garment of praise for the spirit of heaviness, that they might be called trees of righteousness, the planting of the LORD, that He might be glorified.

—ISAIAH 61:2–3

When He was asked by the Pharisees when the kingdom of God would come, He answered them, "The kingdom of God does not come with observation. Nor will they say, 'Here it is!' or 'There it is!' For remember, the kingdom of God is within you."

—LUKE 17:20–21

"After this I will return, and I will rebuild the tabernacle of David, which has fallen. I will rebuild its ruins, and I will set it up, that the rest of men may seek the Lord, and all the Gentiles who are called by My name," says the Lord who does all these things.

—ACTS 15:16–17

When Paul had laid his hands on them, the Holy Spirit came on them, and they spoke in other tongues and prophesied. There were about twelve men in all.

—ACTS 19:6–7

And that you put on the new nature, which was created according to God in righteousness and true holiness.

—EPHESIANS 4:24

But you have come to Mount Zion and to the city of the living God, the heavenly Jerusalem, and to an innumerable company of angels.

—HEBREWS 12:22

MY POSITION AND CALLING

You are the salt of the earth. But if the salt loses its saltiness, how shall it be made salty? It is from then on good for nothing but to be thrown out and to be trampled under foot by men.

—MATTHEW 5:13

You are the light of the world. A city that is set on a hill cannot be hidden.

—MATTHEW 5:14

After the Lord had spoken to them, He was received up into heaven and sat at the right hand of God. Then they went forth and preached everywhere, the Lord working with them and confirming the word through the accompanying signs.

—MARK 16:19–20

So, the Jews persecuted Jesus and sought to kill Him, because He had done these things on the Sabbath day.

—JOHN 5:16

I am the true vine, and My Father is the vinedresser. Every branch in Me that bears no fruit, He takes away. And every branch that bears fruit, He prunes, that it may bear more fruit. You are already clean through the word which I have spoken to you. Remain in Me, as I also remain in you. As the branch cannot bear fruit by itself, unless it remains in the vine, neither can you, unless you remain in Me. I am the vine, you are the branches. He who remains in Me, and I in him, bears much fruit. For without Me you can do nothing.

—JOHN 15:1–5

And having been freed from sin, you became the slaves of righteousness.

—ROMANS 6:18

To the church of God which is at Corinth, to those who are sanctified in Christ Jesus, called to be saints, with all who in every place call on the name of Jesus Christ our Lord, both their Lord and ours.

—1 CORINTHIANS 1:2

Who has made us able ministers of the new covenant, not of the letter but of the Spirit. For the letter kills, but the Spirit gives life.

—2 CORINTHIANS 3:6

Do you not know that you are the temple of God, and that the Spirit of God dwells in you?

—1 CORINTHIANS 3:16

All this is from God, who has reconciled us to Himself through Jesus Christ and has given to us the ministry of reconciliation.

—2 CORINTHIANS 5:18

But he who is joined to the Lord becomes one spirit with Him.

—1 CORINTHIANS 6:17

Now you are the body of Christ and members individually.

—1 Corinthians 12:27

But now in Christ Jesus you who were formerly far away have been brought near by the blood of Christ.

—Ephesians 2:13

For through Him we both have access by one Spirit to the Father.

—Ephesians 2:18

Now, therefore, you are no longer strangers and foreigners, but are fellow-citizens with the saints and members of the household of God.

—Ephesians 2:19

But our citizenship is in heaven, from where also we await for our Savior, the Lord Jesus Christ.

—Philippians 3:20

For you are dead, and your life is hidden with Christ in God.

—Colossians 3:3

When Christ who is our life shall appear, then you also shall appear with Him in glory.

—Colossians 3:4

So embrace, as the elect of God, holy and beloved, a spirit of mercy, kindness, humbleness of mind, meekness, and longsuffering.

—Colossians 3:12

You are all the sons of light and the sons of the day. We are not of the night nor of darkness.

—1 Thessalonians 5:5

You also, as living stones, are being built up into a spiritual house as a holy priesthood to offer up spiritual sacrifices that are acceptable to God through Jesus Christ.

—1 Peter 2:5

Dearly beloved, I implore you as aliens and refugees, abstain from fleshly lusts, which wage war against the soul.

—1 Peter 2:11

Therefore, holy brothers, partakers in a heavenly calling, consider the Apostle and High Priest of our profession, Jesus Christ.

—Hebrews 3:1

My Transformation

For "who has known the mind of the Lord that he may instruct Him"? But we have the mind of Christ.

—1 Corinthians 2:16

Therefore, if any man is in Christ, he is a new creature. Old things have passed away. Look, all things have become new.

—2 Corinthians 5:17

And you are complete in Him, who is the head of all authority and power.

—Colossians 2:10

In Him we have redemption through His blood and the forgiveness of sins according to the riches of His grace. Which He lavished on us in all wisdom and insight.

—Ephesians 1:7–8

For we are His workmanship, created in Christ Jesus for good works, which God prepared beforehand, so that we should walk in them.

—Ephesians 2:10

Even when we were dead in sins, made us alive together with Christ (by grace you have been saved).

—Ephesians 2:5

I have been crucified with Christ. It is no longer I who live, but Christ who lives in me. And the life I now live in the flesh, I live by faith in the Son of God, who loved me and gave Himself for me.

—Galatians 2:20

Truly, truly I say to you, whoever hears My word and believes in Him who sent Me has eternal life and shall not come into condemnation, but has passed from death into life.

—John 5:24

Therefore, since we have been justified by faith, we have peace with God through our Lord Jesus Christ.

—Romans 5:1

For if we have been united with Him in the likeness of His death, so shall we also be united with Him in the likeness of His resurrection. Knowing this, that our old man has been crucified with Him, so that the body of sin might be destroyed, and we should no longer be slaves to sin.

—ROMANS 6:5–6

There is therefore now no condemnation for those who are in Christ Jesus, who walk not according to the flesh, but according to the Spirit.

—ROMANS 8:1

UNDERSTANDING THE ANOINTING

The holy garments belonging to Aaron are to belong to his sons after him, so that they may be anointed in them and be consecrated in them.

—EXODUS 29:29

And I will raise up for Myself a faithful priest, what is in My heart and in My soul he will do it. And I will build him a sure house, and it will walk before My anointed forever.

—1 SAMUEL 2:35

He gives great deliverance to His king, and shows loving-kindness to His anointed, to David and to his descendants for evermore.

—PSALM 18:50

The Spirit of the Lord GOD is upon Me because the LORD has anointed Me to preach good news to the poor. He has sent

Me to heal the brokenhearted, to proclaim liberty to the captives, and the opening of the prison to those who are bound.

—Isaiah 61:1

Truly, truly I say to you, he who believes in Me will do the works that I do also. And he will do greater works than these, because I am going to My Father.

—John 14:12

For he was a good man, full of the Holy Spirit and of faith. And many people were added to the Lord.

—Acts 11:24

But the fruit of the Spirit is love, joy, peace, patience, gentleness, goodness, faith, meekness, and self-control; against such there is no law.

—Galatians 5:22–23

I thank Christ Jesus our Lord who has enabled me, because He counted me faithful and appointed me to the ministry.

—1 Timothy 1:12

You lust and do not have, so you kill. You desire to have and cannot obtain. You fight and war. Yet you do not have, because you do not ask.

—James 4:2

But you have an anointing from the Holy One, and you know all things. I have written to you, not because you do not know the truth, but because you know it, and because no lie is of the truth. Who is a liar but the one who denies that Jesus is the Christ? Whoever denies the Father and the Son is the antichrist.

—1 John 2:20–22

JOINT HEIRS IN CHRIST

That which is born of the flesh is flesh, and that which is born of the Spirit is spirit.

—John 3:6

He who believes in Him is not condemned. But he who does not believe is condemned already, because he has not believed in the name of the only begotten Son of God.

—John 3:18

By this He spoke of the Spirit, whom those who believe in Him would receive. For the Holy Spirit was not yet given, because Jesus was not yet glorified.

—John 7:39

This righteousness of God comes through faith in Jesus Christ to all and upon all who believe, for there is no distinction.

—Romans 3:22

Therefore, since we have been justified by faith, we have peace with God through our Lord Jesus Christ, through whom we also have access by faith into this grace in which we stand, and so we rejoice in hope of the glory of God.

—Romans 5:1–2

For sin shall not have dominion over you, for you are not under the law, but under grace.

—ROMANS 6:14

So, my brothers, you also have died to the law through the body of Christ, so that you may be married to another, to Him who has been raised from the dead, so that we may bear fruit for God.

—ROMANS 7:4

You, however, are not in the flesh but in the Spirit, if indeed the Spirit of God lives in you. Now if any man does not have the Spirit of Christ, he does not belong to Him.

—ROMANS 8:9

But if the Spirit of Him who raised Jesus from the dead lives in you, He who raised Christ from the dead will also give life to your mortal bodies through His Spirit that lives in you.

—ROMANS 8:11

No, in all these things we are more than conquerors through Him who loved us.

—ROMANS 8:37

God is faithful, and by Him you were called to the fellowship of His Son, Jesus Christ our Lord.

—1 CORINTHIANS 1:9

But because of Him you are in Christ Jesus, whom God made unto us wisdom, righteousness, sanctification, and redemption.

—1 CORINTHIANS 1:30

For no one can lay another foundation than that which was laid, which is Jesus Christ.

—1 CORINTHIANS 3:11

You were bought with a price. Therefore glorify God in your body and in your spirit, which are God's.

—1 CORINTHIANS 6:20

Such were some of you. But you were washed, you were sanctified, and you were justified in the name of the Lord Jesus by the Spirit of our God.

—1 CORINTHIANS 6:11

And all drank the same spiritual drink, for they drank of that spiritual Rock that followed them, and that Rock was Christ.

—1 CORINTHIANS 10:4

But that one and very same Spirit works all these, dividing to each one individually as He will.

—1 CORINTHIANS 12:11

For by one Spirit we are all baptized into one body, whether we are Jews or Gentiles, whether we are slaves or free, and we have all been made to drink of one Spirit.

—1 CORINTHIANS 12:13

To an incorruptible and undefiled inheritance that does not fade away, kept in heaven for you.

—1 Peter 1:4

Who also has sealed us and established the guarantee with the Spirit in our hearts.

—2 Corinthians 1:22

God made Him who knew no sin to be sin for us, that we might become the righteousness of God in Him.

—2 Corinthians 5:21

Now He who supplies seed to the sower and supplies bread for your food will also multiply your seed sown and increase the fruits of your righteousness. So you will be enriched in everything to all bountifulness, which makes us give thanks to God.

—2 Corinthians 9:10–11

But now that faith has come, we are no longer under a tutor.

—Galatians 3:25

You are all sons of God by faith in Christ Jesus.

—Galatians 3:26

And what is the surpassing greatness of His power toward us who believe, according to the working of His mighty power.

—Ephesians 1:19

He predestined us to adoption as sons to Himself through Jesus Christ according to the good pleasure of His will.

—Ephesians 1:5

But God, being rich in mercy, because of His great love with which He loved us.

—Ephesians 2:4

Having been built upon the foundation of the apostles and prophets, Jesus Christ Himself being the chief cornerstone.

—Ephesians 2:20

Husbands, love your wives, just as Christ also loved the church and gave Himself for it, that He might sanctify and cleanse it with the washing of water by the word, and that He might present to Himself a glorious church, not having spot, or wrinkle, or any such thing, but that it should be holy and without blemish.

—Ephesians 5:25–27

For God is the One working in you, both to will and to do His good pleasure.

—Philippians 2:13

And be found in Him, not having my own righteousness which is from the law, but that which is through faith in Christ, the righteousness which is of God on the basis of faith.

—Philippians 3:9

In Him you were also circumcised by putting off the body of the sinful nature, not a circumcision performed with hands, but by the circumcision performed by Christ.

—Colossians 2:11

Bear with one another and forgive one another. If anyone has a quarrel against anyone, even as Christ forgave you, so you must do.

—Colossians 3:13

Knowing that from the Lord you will receive the reward of the inheritance. For you serve the Lord Christ.

—Colossians 3:24

Paul, Silas, and Timothy, to the church of the Thessalonians which is in God the Father and in the Lord Jesus Christ: Grace to you and peace from God our Father and the Lord Jesus Christ.

—1 Thessalonians 1:1

For you know that you were not redeemed from your vain way of life inherited from your fathers with perishable things, like silver or gold, but with the precious blood of Christ, as of a lamb without blemish and without spot.

—1 Peter 1:18–19

For you have been born again, not from perishable seed, but imperishable, through the living and eternal word of God.

—1 Peter 1:23

But you are a chosen people, a royal priesthood, a holy nation, a people for God's own possession, so that you may declare the goodness of Him who has called you out of darkness into His marvelous light.

—1 Peter 2:9

Grace and peace be multiplied to you through the knowledge of God and of Jesus our Lord.

—2 PETER 1:2

If we confess our sins, He is faithful and just to forgive us our sins and cleanse us from all unrighteousness.

—1 JOHN 1:9

But the anointing which you have received from Him remains in you, and you do not need anyone to teach you. For as the same anointing teaches you concerning all things, and is truth, and is no lie, and just as it has taught you, remain in Him.

—1 JOHN 2:27

Now the one who keeps His commandments remains in Him, and He in him. And by this we know that He remains in us, through the Spirit whom He has given us.

—1 JOHN 3:24

KINGDOM PRINCIPLES

Now then, you kings, be wise. Be admonished, you judges of the earth. Serve the LORD with fear, tremble with trepidation!

—PSALM 2:10–11

All the ends of the world will remember and turn to the LORD; and all the families of the nations will worship before You. For kingship belongs to the LORD, and He rules among the nations.

—PSALM 22:27–28

Delight yourself in the LORD, and He will give you the desires of your heart. Commit your way to the LORD; trust also in Him, and He will bring it to pass. He will bring forth your righteousness as the light, and your judgment as the noonday.
—Psalm 37:4–6

In God I trust, I will not fear; what can a man do to me? Your vows are on me, O God; I will complete them with thank offerings to You.
—Psalm 56:11–12

All the earth will worship You and will sing to You; they will sing to Your name. Selah.
—Psalm 66:4

That Your way may be known on earth, Your salvation among all nations.
—Psalm 67:2

All nations whom You have made shall come and worship before You, O Lord, and shall glorify Your name.
—Psalm 86:9

The LORD has established His throne in the heavens, and His kingdom rules over all.
—Psalm 103:19

For the LORD has chosen Zion; He has desired it for His dwelling. "This is My resting place forever; here I will dwell, for I have chosen it."
—Psalm 132:13–14

Your kingdom is an everlasting kingdom, and Your dominion endures throughout all generations.

—PSALM 145:13

For unto us a child is born, unto us a son is given, and the government shall be upon his shoulder. And his name shall be called Wonderful Counselor, Mighty God, Eternal Father, Prince of Peace.

—ISAIAH 9:6

Drip down, O heavens, from above, and let the clouds pour down righteousness. Let the earth open up, and let them bring forth salvation, and let righteousness spring up together. I the LORD have created it.

—ISAIAH 45:8

Surely you shall call a nation that you do not know, and nations that did not know you shall run to you because of the LORD your God, even the Holy One of Israel. For He has glorified you.

—ISAIAH 55:5

The Gentiles shall see your righteousness, and all kings your glory. And you shall be called by a new name, which the mouth of the LORD shall name.

—ISAIAH 62:2

"But let him who glories glory in this, that he understands and knows Me, that I am the LORD who exercises lovingkindness, justice, and righteousness in the earth. For in these things I delight," says the LORD.

—JEREMIAH 9:24

The LORD has taken away your judgments; He has cast out your enemies. The King of Israel, the LORD, is in your midst; you will see evil no more.

—ZEPHANIAH 3:15

Do not store up for yourselves treasures on earth where moth and rust destroy and where thieves break in and steal.

—MATTHEW 6:19

For the kingdom of God does not mean eating and drinking, but righteousness and peace and joy in the Holy Spirit.

—ROMANS 14:17

Therefore judge nothing before the appointed time until the Lord comes. He will bring to light the hidden things of darkness and will reveal the purposes of the hearts. Then everyone will have commendation from God.

—1 CORINTHIANS 4:5

To them God would make known what is the glorious riches of this mystery among the nations. It is Christ in you, the hope of glory.

—COLOSSIANS 1:27

If we endure, we shall also reign with Him; if we deny Him, He also will deny us.

—2 TIMOTHY 2:12

But you have come to Mount Zion and to the city of the living God, the heavenly Jerusalem, and to an innumerable company of angels.

—HEBREWS 12:22

That if you confess with your mouth Jesus is Lord, and believe in your heart that God has raised Him from the dead, you will be saved, for with the heart one believes unto righteousness, and with the mouth confession is made unto salvation.

—ROMANS 10:9–10

Therefore let us pursue the things which produce peace and the things that build up one another. Do not destroy the work of God for the sake of food. All things indeed are clean, but it is evil for the man who causes someone to fall by what he eats.

—ROMANS 14:19–20

And that the Gentiles might glorify God for His mercy. As it is written, "For this reason I will acknowledge You among the Gentiles, and I will sing praises to Your name."

—ROMANS 15:9

GOD'S BLESSINGS ON THE KINGDOM

The LORD said to Moses, "I will do this thing of which you have spoken, for you have found favor in My sight, and I know you by name." Then Moses said, "I pray, show me Your glory."

—EXODUS 33:17–18

The Lord passed by before him, and proclaimed, "The Lord, the Lord God, merciful and gracious, slow to anger, and abounding in goodness and truth, keeping mercy for thousands, forgiving iniquity and transgression and sin, but who will by no means clear the guilty, visiting the iniquity of fathers on the children and on the children's children, to the third and fourth generation."

—Exodus 34:6–7

The Lord bless you and keep you! The Lord make His face to shine upon you, and be gracious unto you. The Lord lift His face countenance upon you, and give you peace.

—Numbers 6:24–26

Whenever you reap your harvest in your field and have forgotten a sheaf in the field, you may not go back to get it. It will be for the foreigner, for the fatherless, and for the widow, so that the Lord your God may bless you in all the work of your hands. When you beat your olive tree, you may not go over the boughs again. It will be for the foreigner, for the fatherless, and for the widow. When you gather the grapes of your vineyard, you shall not glean it again. It will be for the foreigner, for the fatherless, and for the widow.

—Deuteronomy 24:19–21

Bless, O Lord, his substance, and accept the work of his hands. Run through the loins of them that rise against him and of them that hate him, so that they rise never again.

—Deuteronomy 33:11

Then Jabez called on the God of Israel, saying, "Oh that You would indeed bless me and enlarge my territory, that Your hand might be with me, and that You would keep me from evil, that it may not bring me hardship!" So God granted what he asked.

—1 Chronicles 4:10

Show marvelously Your lovingkindness, O Deliverer of those who seek refuge by Your right hand from those who arise in opposition.

—Psalm 17:7

Your word I have hidden in my heart, that I might not sin against You. Blessed are You, O Lord; teach me Your statutes.

—Psalm 119:11–12

Surely goodness and mercy will follow me all the days of my life, and I will dwell in the house of the Lord forever.

— Psalm 23:6

Your mercy, O Lord, is in the heavens, and Your faithfulness reaches to the clouds. Your righteousness is like the great mountains; Your judgments like the great deep; O Lord, You preserve man and beast.

—Psalm 36:5–6

Be my rock of refuge to enter continually; You have given commandment to save me; for You are my rock and my stronghold.

—Psalm 71:3

A good name is rather to be chosen than great riches, and loving favor rather than silver and gold.

—PROVERBS 22:1

Trust in the LORD with all your heart, and lean not on your own understanding. In all your ways acknowledge Him, and He will direct your paths.

—PROVERBS 3:5–6

Do not remember the former things nor consider the things of old. See, I will do a new thing. Now it shall spring forth. Shall you not be aware of it? I will even make a way in the wilderness, and rivers in the desert.

—ISAIAH 43:18–19

The glory of Lebanon shall come to you, the fir tree, the pine tree, and the box tree together, to beautify the place of My sanctuary. And I will make the place of My feet glorious.

—ISAIAH 60:13

And I brought you into a plentiful country to eat its fruit and its goodness. But when you entered, you defiled My land and made My heritage an abomination.

—JEREMIAH 2:7

O LORD, are not Your eyes upon the truth? You have stricken them, but they have not grieved. You have consumed them, but they have refused to receive correction. They have made their faces harder than a rock. They have refused to return.

—JEREMIAH 5:3

I am the good shepherd. I know My sheep, and am known by My own. Even as the Father knows Me, so I know the Father. And I lay down My life for the sheep. I have other sheep who are not of this fold. I must also bring them, and they will hear My voice. There will be one flock and one shepherd.

—John 10:14–16

And delivered him out of all his afflictions, and gave him favor and wisdom before Pharaoh, king of Egypt, who appointed him governor over Egypt and all his house. Then a famine came over all Egypt and Canaan with great affliction, and our fathers found no sustenance.

—Acts 7:10–11

So they continued there a long time, speaking boldly for the Lord, who bore witness to His gracious word, granting signs and wonders to be done by their hands.

—Acts 14:3

But God has revealed them to us by His Spirit. For the Spirit searches all things, yes, the deep things of God.

—1 Corinthians 2:10

Blessed be God, the Father of our Lord Jesus Christ, the Father of mercies, and the God of all comfort, who comforts us in all our tribulation, that we may be able to comfort those who are in any trouble by the comfort with which we ourselves are comforted by God. As the sufferings of Christ abound in us, so our consolation also abounds through Christ.

—2 Corinthians 1:3–5

Just as He chose us in Him before the foundation of the world, to be holy and blameless before Him in love.

—Ephesians 1:4

For every house is built by someone, but the One who builds all things is God. Moses was faithful in all God's house as a servant, testifying about those things that were to be spoken later. But Christ is faithful over God's house as a Son, whose house we are if we firmly hold our confidence and the rejoicing of our hope to the end.

—Hebrews 3:4–6

"Our God is Jehovah of hosts, who can summon unexpected reinforcements at any moment to aid His people. Believe that He is there between you and your difficulty, and what baffles you will flee before Him, as clouds before the gale."

F. B. MEYER

Chapter 8

ARMED AND DANGEROUS

GOD'S FAVOR

Esau said, "What do you mean by all this company that I met?" Jacob answered, "These are to find favor in the sight of my lord."

—GENESIS 33:8

When the time drew near when Israel would die, he called his son Joseph and said to him, "If now I have found grace in your sight, please put your hand under my thigh and deal kindly and truly with me. Please do not bury me in Egypt."

—GENESIS 47:29

For You, LORD, will bless the righteous. You surround him with favor like a shield.

—PSALM 5:12

But You, O LORD, be gracious to me, and raise me up, that I may repay them.

—PSALM 41:10

LORD, you have been favorable to Your land; You have brought back the captivity of Jacob.

—PSALM 85:1

For whoever finds me finds life, and will obtain favor of the LORD.

—PROVERBS 8:35

In the light of the king's countenance is life, and his favor is as a cloud of the latter rain.

—Proverbs 16:15

For the weapons of our warfare are not carnal, but mighty through God to the pulling down of strongholds.

—2 Corinthians 10:4

Blessed be the God and Father of our Lord Jesus Christ, who has blessed us with every spiritual blessing in the heavenly places in Christ.

—Ephesians 1:3

Having your feet fitted with the readiness of the gospel of peace, and above all, taking the shield of faith, with which you will be able to extinguish all the fiery arrows of the evil one. Take the helmet of salvation and the sword of the Spirit, which is the word of God.

—Ephesians 6:15–17

God's Safety

The desire of the humble You have heard, O Lord; You make their heart attentive. You bend Your ear to judge the orphan and the oppressed. Man on earth no longer trembles.

—Psalm 10:17–18

"Because the poor are plundered, because the needy sigh, now I will arise," says the Lord. "I will place him in the safety for which he yearns."

—Psalm 12:5

O taste and see that the LORD is good; blessed is the one who seeks refuge in Him.

—PSALM 34:8

Then He led out His own people like sheep and guided them in the wilderness like a flock.

—PSALM 78:52

Great is our Lord and great in power; His understanding is without measure. The LORD lifts up the meek; He casts the wicked down to the ground.

—PSALM 147:5–6

For thus says the High and Lofty One who inhabits eternity, whose name is Holy, "I dwell in the high and holy place and also with him who is of a contrite and humble spirit, to revive the spirit of the humble, and to revive the heart of the contrite ones."

—ISAIAH 57:15

GARMENT OF RIGHTEOUSNESS

"Now when I passed by you and looked upon you, you were old enough for love. So I spread My garment over you and covered your nakedness. Indeed, I swore to you, and entered into a covenant with you," says the Lord GOD, "and you became Mine."

—EZEKIEL 16:8

For You have turned my mourning into dancing; You have put off my sackcloth and girded me with gladness, so that my glory may sing praise to You and not be silent. O Lᴏʀᴅ my God, I will give thanks to You forever.

—Psᴀʟᴍ 30:11–12

I will greatly rejoice in the Lᴏʀᴅ, my soul shall be joyful in my God. For He has clothed me with the garments of salvation. He has covered me with the robe of righteousness, as a bridegroom decks himself with ornaments, and as a bride adorns herself with her jewels.

—Isᴀɪᴀʜ 61:10

But the father said to his servants, "Bring out the best robe and put it on him. And put a ring on his hand and shoes on his feet."

—Lᴜᴋᴇ 15:22

Stand therefore, having your waist girded with truth, having put on the breastplate of righteousness.

—Eᴘʜᴇsɪᴀɴs 6:14

Dᴇʟɪᴠᴇʀᴇᴅ Fʀᴏᴍ Wɪᴄᴋᴇᴅɴᴇss

Your servant has found grace in your eyes, and you have shown your mercy, which you have shown to me by saving my life. However, I cannot escape to the mountain. Otherwise some evil will overtake me, and I will die.

—Gᴇɴᴇsɪs 19:19

And I will appoint a place for My people Israel, and I will plant them there where they will dwell securely and tremble no more, so that the sons of wickedness will not oppress them just as before.

—1 Chronicles 17:9

For the Lord knows the way of the righteous, but the way of the ungodly will perish.

—Psalm 1:6

For they intended evil against You; they devised evil thoughts, they will not be able to accomplish.

—Psalm 21:11

The eyes of the Lord are on the righteous, and His ears are open to their cry. The face of the Lord is against the ones doing evil, to cut off the memory of them from the earth. The righteous cry, and the Lord hears, and delivers them out of all their troubles.

—Psalm 34:15–17

Hear my voice, O God, in my complaint; guard my life from dread of the enemy. Hide me from the secret counsel of the wicked, from the throng of workers of iniquity.

—Psalm 64:1–2

He delivered us from so great a death and does deliver us. In Him we trust that He will still deliver us.

—2 Corinthians 1:10

And do not have fellowship with the unfruitful works of darkness; instead, expose them. For it is shameful even to speak of those things which are done by them in secret. But all things are exposed when they are revealed by the light, for everything that becomes visible is light.

—Ephesians 5:11–13

He has delivered us from the power of darkness and has transferred us into the kingdom of His dear Son.

—Colossians 1:13

Let us then come with confidence to the throne of grace, that we may obtain mercy and find grace to help in time of need.

—Hebrews 4:16

Warfare Prayers

They shall no more offer their sacrifices to goat demons, after whom they have acted like whores. This shall be a perpetual statute for them throughout their generations.

—Leviticus 17:7

So the people entered the city by stealth that day, as a people who have been disgraced steal away when they flee from battle.

—2 Samuel 19:3

When Rehoboam came to Jerusalem, he called together from the house of Judah and Benjamin one hundred and eighty thousand choice men to make war and to battle with Israel in order to restore the kingdom to Rehoboam.

—2 Chronicles 11:1

The LORD also thundered in the heavens, and the Most High gave His voice, hailstones and coals of fire.

—PSALM 18:13

He delivered me from my strong enemy, and from those who hated me, for they were too strong for me.

—PSALM 18:17

I pursued my enemies and overtook them; I did not return until they were destroyed.

—PSALM 18:37

You gave me the necks of my enemies, and I destroyed those who hate me.

—PSALM 18:40

Whose mouth speaks lies, and their right hand is a right hand of falsehood.

—PSALM 144:8

Blessed be the LORD my strength, who prepares my hands for war, and my fingers to fight.

—PSALM 144:1

All you beasts of the field, all you beasts in the forest, come to devour.

—ISAIAH 56:9

For by fire and by His sword on all flesh, the LORD shall execute judgment. And the slain of the LORD shall be many. "Those who sanctify themselves and purify themselves in the gardens behind one tree in the midst, eating swine's flesh, and abominable things, and mice shall be consumed together," says the LORD.

—ISAIAH 66:16–17

Let a cry be heard from their houses, when You bring a troop suddenly upon them; for they have dug a pit to take me and hidden snares for my feet.

—JEREMIAH 18:22

"Arise and thresh, daughter of Zion, for I will make your horn iron, your hoofs I will make bronze, and you will shatter many peoples." I will devote their pillage to the LORD, their wealth to the LORD of all the earth.

—MICAH 4:13

"And you will tread down the wicked, for they will be ashes under the soles of your feet, on the day when I do this," says the LORD of Hosts.

—MALACHI 4:3

When He came to the other side into the country of the Gergesenes, there met Him two men possessed with demons, coming out of the tombs, extremely fierce, so that no one might pass by that way.

—MATTHEW 8:28

Then He said to her, "For this answer, go your way. The demon has gone out of your daughter."

—MARK 7:29

Jesus answered them, "Have I not chosen you, the twelve, and yet one of you is a devil?"

—John 6:70

But I say that the things which the Gentiles sacrifice, they sacrifice to demons, and not to God. I do not want you to have fellowship with demons.

—1 Corinthians 10:20

For though we walk in the flesh, we do not war according to the flesh.

—2 Corinthians 10:3

For such are false apostles and deceitful workers, disguising themselves as apostles of Christ.

—2 Corinthians 11:13

In journeys often, in perils of waters, in perils of robbers, in perils by my own countrymen, in perils by the Gentiles, in perils in the city, in perils in the wilderness, in perils in the sea, in perils among false brothers.

—2 Corinthians 11:26

Now the Spirit clearly says that in the last times some will depart from the faith and pay attention to seducing spirits and doctrines of devils.

—1 Timothy 4:1

For God has not given us the spirit of fear, but of power, and love, and self-control.

—2 Timothy 1:7

You are of God, little children, and have overcome them, because He who is in you is greater than he who is in the world.

—1 John 4:4

Little children, keep yourselves from idols. Amen.

—1 John 5:21

Then war broke out in heaven. Michael and his angels fought against the dragon, and the dragon and his angels fought.

—Revelation 12:7

ARMING FOR VICTORY

Only do not rebel against the Lord, nor fear the people of the land because they are bread for us. Their defense is gone from them, and the Lord is with us. Do not fear them.

—Numbers 14:9

Out of all your gifts you shall present every offering due to the Lord, from all the best of them, the consecrated part of them.

—Numbers 18:29

A man who is clean will gather the ashes of the heifer and deposit them outside the camp in a clean place, and it will be guarded for the assembly of the Israelites for water of purification. It is for purifying from sin.

—Numbers 19:9

The Lord will make you the head and not the tail, and you will only be above and you will not be beneath, if you listen to the commandments of the Lord your God, which I am commanding you today, to observe and to do them.

—Deuteronomy 28:13

The men of David said to him, "This is the day of which the Lord said to you, 'I am giving your enemy into your hand. You may do with him as seems good in your eyes.'" Then David arose and secretly cut off the corner of Saul's robe.

—1 Samuel 24:4

But if you go, do it. Be strong for the battle. Yet, God shall make you fall before the enemy, for God has power to help and to bring down.

—2 Chronicles 25:8

He who sits in the heavens laughs, the Lord ridicules them.

—Psalm 2:4

I will declare the decree of the Lord. He said to Me, "You are My Son; this day have I begotten You. Ask of Me, and I will give You the nations for Your inheritance, and the ends of the earth for Your possession."

—Psalm 2:7–8

Take note and answer me, O Lord my God! Brighten my eyes, lest I sleep the sleep of death, lest my enemy say, "I have him," lest my foes exult when I stumble.

—Psalm 13:3–4

You will make known to me the path of life; in Your presence is fullness of joy; at Your right hand there are pleasures for evermore.

—PSALM 16:11

And have not delivered me up into the hand of the enemy; You have set my feet in a broad place.

—PSALM 31:8

By this I know that You favor me, because my enemy does not triumph over me.

—PSALM 41:11

From the voice of him who reproaches and reviles, by reason of the enemy and avenger.

—PSALM 44:16

The God of lovingkindness will go before me; God will cause me to look triumphantly on my foes.

—PSALM 59:10

For You have been a refuge for me, and a strong tower from the enemy.

—PSALM 61:3

For I was envious at the boastful, I saw the prosperity of the wicked. For there are no pains in their death; their bodies are fat.

—PSALM 73:3–4

O God, how long will the adversary scorn? Will the enemy blaspheme Your name forever?

—PSALM 74:10

For the LORD God is a sun and shield; the LORD will give favor and glory, for no good thing will He withhold from the one who walks uprightly.

—PSALM 84:11

I will sing of the mercies of the LORD forever; with my mouth I will make known Your faithfulness to all generations. For I have said, "Mercy shall be built up forever; Your faithfulness shall be established in the heavens."

—PSALM 89:1–2

You have broken down all his walls; You have brought his strongholds to ruin.

—PSALM 89:40

You have also turned back the edge of his sword and have not made him stand in battle. You have made his glory cease and cast his throne down to the ground.

—PSALM 89:43–44

He shall cover you with his feathers, and under His wings you shall find protection; His faithfulness shall be your shield and wall.

—PSALM 91:4

You shall tread upon the lion and adder; the young lion and the serpent you shall trample underfoot.

—PSALM 91:13

Our fathers did not consider Your wonders in Egypt; they did not remember the greatness of Your mercy, but rebelled against Him at the sea, by the Red Sea. Nevertheless He saved them for His name's sake, that He might make His mighty power known.

—PSALM 106:7–8

Your faithfulness is for all generations; You have established the earth, and it is firm.

—PSALM 119:90

Let the proud be ashamed, for they have been wicked to me in falsehood, but I will meditate on Your precepts.

—PSALM 119:78

Grant not, O LORD, the desires of the wicked; do not allow his evil plot, lest he be raised up. Selah. As for the head of those who encompass me, let the mischief of their own lips overwhelm them. Let burning coals fall upon them; let them be cast into the fire, into deep pits that they do not rise up again.

—PSALM 140:8–10

The name of the LORD is a strong tower; the righteous run into it and are safe.

—PROVERBS 18:10

Do not rejoice when your enemy falls, and do not let your heart be glad when he stumbles.

—Proverbs 24:17

The north wind brings rain, and a backbiting tongue an angry countenance.

—Proverbs 25:23

Where there is no vision, the people perish; but happy is he who keeps the teaching.

—Proverbs 29:18

The one who digs a pit will fall into it, and the one who breaks through a wall will be bitten by a serpent.

—Ecclesiastes 10:8

When they say to you, "Seek after the mediums and the wizards, who whisper and mutter," should not a people seek after their God? Should they consult the dead for the living? To the law and to the testimony, if they do not speak according to this word, it is because there is no light in them.

—Isaiah 8:19–20

O Lord, You are my God. I will exalt You, I will praise Your name, for You have done wonderful things. Your plans formed of old are faithfulness and truth. For You have made a city into a heap, a fortified city into a ruin. A palace of strangers is a city no longer. It shall never be built. Therefore a strong people shall glorify You. Cities of ruthless nations shall fear You.

—Isaiah 25:1–3

Let the wicked forsake his way, and the unrighteous man his thoughts. And let him return to the LORD, and He will have mercy upon him, and to our God, for He will abundantly pardon.

—ISAIAH 55:7

For thus says the LORD of Hosts, the God of Israel, "Do not let your prophets and your diviners who are in your midst deceive you, and do not listen to the dreams which they dream."

—JEREMIAH 29:8

Therefore a lion out of the forest will slay them, and a wolf from the deserts will destroy them, a leopard will watch over their cities. Everyone who goes out from there will be torn in pieces. Because their transgressions are many and their backslidings have increased.

—JEREMIAH 5:6

Declare among the nations and publish, and set up a standard. Do not conceal it but say, "Babylon has been captured. Bel has been humiliated. Marduk has been broken in pieces. Her idols have been humiliated. Her images have been broken in pieces."

—JEREMIAH 50:2

"Thus shall they know that I, the LORD their God, am with them, and that they, the house of Israel, are My people," says the Lord GOD.

—EZEKIEL 34:30

Therefore whoever resists the authority resists what God has appointed, and those who resist will incur judgment.

—Romans 13:2

Your obedience has become known to all men. Therefore I am glad on your behalf. Yet, I want you to be wise to that which is good, and innocent to that which is evil. The God of peace will soon crush Satan under your feet. The grace of our Lord Jesus Christ be with you.

—Romans 16:19–20

For the weapons of our warfare are not carnal, but mighty through God to the pulling down of strongholds, casting down imaginations and every high thing that exalts itself against the knowledge of God, bringing every thought into captivity to the obedience of Christ.

—2 Corinthians 10:4–5

Therefore take up the whole armor of God that you may be able to resist in the evil day, and having done all, to stand.

—Ephesians 6:13

Rejoice always. Pray without ceasing. In everything give thanks, for this is the will of God in Christ Jesus concerning you.

—1 Thessalonians 5:16–18

But the Lord is faithful, who will establish you and guard you from the evil one.

—2 Thessalonians 3:3

But those who desire to be rich fall into temptation and a snare and into many foolish and harmful lusts, which drown men in ruin and destruction. For the love of money is the root of all evil. While coveting after money, some have strayed from the faith and pierced themselves through with many sorrows.

—1 TIMOTHY 6:9–10

Let not that man think that he will receive anything from the Lord. A double-minded man is unstable in all his ways.

—JAMES 1:7–8

Draw near to God, and He will draw near to you. Cleanse your hands, you sinners, and purify your hearts, you double-minded.

—JAMES 4:8

My little children, I am writing these things to you, so that you do not sin. But if anyone does sin, we have an Advocate with the Father, Jesus Christ the Righteous One.

—1 JOHN 2:1

Beloved, if our heart does not condemn us, then we have confidence before God. And whatever we ask, we will receive from Him, because we keep His commandments and do the things that are pleasing in His sight.

—1 JOHN 3:21–22

But you, beloved, build yourselves up in your most holy faith. Pray in the Holy Spirit.

—JUDE 20

WALKING IN GOD'S WAYS

The young lions are in want and suffer hunger, but the ones who seek the LORD will not lack any good thing.

—PSALM 34:10

May there be abundance of grain in the earth on the top of the mountains; may its fruit shake like Lebanon; and may those from the city flourish like grass of the earth.

—PSALM 72:16

I will say of the LORD, "He is my refuge and my fortress, my God in whom I trust." Surely He shall deliver you from the snare of the hunter and from the deadly pestilence.

—PSALM 91:2–3

The righteous shall flourish like the palm tree and grow like a cedar in Lebanon.

—PSALM 92:12

Many people shall go and say, "Come, and let us go up to the mountain of the LORD, to the house of the God of Jacob, and He will teach us of His ways, and we will walk in His paths." For out of Zion shall go forth the law, and the word of the LORD from Jerusalem.

—ISAIAH 2:3

He who walks righteously and speaks uprightly. He who rejects unjust gain and shakes his hands from holding bribes, who stops his ears from hearing of bloodshed, and shuts his eyes from seeing evil. He shall dwell on high. His place of defense shall be the impregnable rock. His bread shall be given him. His waters shall be sure.

—ISAIAH 33:15–16

But this thing I commanded them, saying, "Obey My voice, and I will be your God, and you shall be My people. And walk in all the ways that I have commanded you, that it may be well with you."

—JEREMIAH 7:23

"Bring all the tithes into the storehouse, that there may be food in My house, and test Me now in this," says the Lord of Hosts, "if I will not open for you the windows of heaven and pour out for you a blessing, that there will not be room enough to receive it."

—MALACHI 3:10

For whoever does the will of My Father who is in heaven is My brother, and sister, and mother.

—MATTHEW 12:50

See then that you walk carefully, not as fools, but as wise men.

—EPHESIANS 5:15

For you were formerly darkness, but now you are light in the Lord. Walk as children of light.

—EPHESIANS 5:8

Walk in wisdom toward those who are outside, wisely using the opportunity.

—Colossians 4:5

So that you may walk honestly toward those who are outsiders and that you may lack nothing.

—1 Thessalonians 4:12

By this we know that we love the children of God: when we love God and keep His commandments. For this is the love of God, that we keep His commandments. And His commandments are not burdensome.

—1 John 5:2–3

So faith by itself, if it has no works, is dead.

—James 2:17

Demonic Spirits of Old and New Testaments

Jealous spirit

And the spirit of jealousy comes on him, and he is jealous of his wife, and she is defiled, or if the spirit of jealousy comes on him, and he is jealous of his wife, and she is not defiled.

—Numbers 5:14

Evil spirit

Now the Spirit of the Lord departed from Saul and an evil spirit from the Lord terrified him. So the servants of Saul said to him, "See, an evil spirit from God troubles you. Let our lord now tell your servants, who are before you, that they might seek out a man experienced in playing the lyre. And it will come to pass, when the evil spirit from God is on you, that he will play with his hand, and you will be well."

—1 Samuel 16:14–16

Lying spirit

The Lord said to him, "How?" And he said, "I will go and be a lying spirit in the mouth of all his prophets." And He said, "You will be successful and persuade him. Go forth, and do so."

—1 Kings 22:22

Spirit of Cyrus

In the first year of King Cyrus of Persia, that the word of the Lord spoken by the mouth of Jeremiah might be fulfilled, the Lord stirred up the spirit of King Cyrus of Persia, so that he sent a proclamation throughout all his kingdom and also declared in a written edict.

—2 Chronicles 36:22

Broken spirit

A merry heart does good like a medicine, but a broken spirit dries the bones.

—Proverbs 17:22

Wounded spirit

The spirit of a man will sustain his infirmity, but a wounded spirit who can bear?

—Proverbs 18:14

Haughty, rebellious spirit

The end of a matter is better than the beginning of it, and the patient in spirit than the haughty in spirit.

—Ecclesiastes 7:8

Spirit of Egypt

The spirit of Egypt shall be discouraged in their midst, and I will destroy their counsel. Then they shall seek for the idols and for the charmers and for the mediums and the sorcerers.

—Isaiah 19:3

Spirit of deep sleep

For the Lord has poured out on you the spirit of deep sleep and has closed your eyes, the prophets. And He has covered your heads, the seers.

—Isaiah 29:10

Destroying spirit

Thus says the Lord, "I will raise up against Babylon and against those who dwell in Lebkamai, the spirit of a destroyer."

—Jeremiah 51:1

Spirit of the kings of Medes

Sharpen the arrows. Gather the shields. The LORD has raised up the spirit of the kings of the Medes. For His device is against Babylon, to destroy it; because it is the vengeance of the LORD, the vengeance of His temple.

—JEREMIAH 51:11

One's own human spirit

Thus says the Lord GOD, "Woe to the foolish prophets who follow their own spirit and have seen nothing!"

—EZEKIEL 13:3

Spirit of harlotry

Swearing, lying, and killing, and stealing and adultery break out, and bloodshed follows bloodshed....I know Ephraim, and Israel is not hidden from Me, for now, O Ephraim, you have played the whore.

—HOSEA 4:2, 5:3

Spirit of falsehood

If a man, going about vapidly and deceitfully, lies, "I will preach for you wine and beer," he would be just the preacher for this people.

—MICAH 2:11

Unclean spirit

"And on that day," says the LORD of Hosts, "I will cut off the names of the idols from the land, and they will not be remembered any more. And I will also remove from the land the prophets and the unclean spirit."

—ZECHARIAH 13:2

Foul, deaf, dumb spirit

When Jesus saw that the people came running together, He rebuked the foul spirit, saying to it, "You mute and deaf spirit, I command you, come out of him, and enter him no more."

—MARK 9:25

Spirit of unclean demon

In the synagogue there was a man who had the spirit of an unclean demon. And he cried out with a loud voice, "Leave us alone! What have You to do with us, Jesus of Nazareth? Have You come to destroy us? I know who You are—the Holy One of God!"

—LUKE 4:33–34

Spirit of infirmity

And there was a woman who had a spirit of infirmity for eighteen years and was bent over and could not straighten herself up.

—LUKE 13:11

Spirit of the antichrist

And every spirit that does not confess that Jesus Christ has come in the flesh is not from God. This is the spirit of the antichrist, which you have heard is coming and is already in the world.

—1 John 4:3

Spirit of divination

On one occasion, as we went to the place of prayer, a servant girl possessed with a spirit of divination met us, who brought her masters much profit by fortune-telling.

—Acts 16:16

Spirit of lust

Therefore God gave them up to uncleanness through the lusts of their hearts, to dishonor their own bodies among themselves.

—Romans 1:24

Spirit of bondage

For you have not received the spirit of slavery again to fear. But you have received the Spirit of adoption, by whom we cry, "Abba, Father."

—Romans 8:15

Spirit of slumber

As it is written, "God has given them a spirit of slumber, eyes that would not see and ears that would not hear, to this very day."

—Romans 11:8

Spirit of man

For what man knows the things of a man, except the spirit of man which is in him? Likewise, no one knows the things of God, except the Spirit of God.

—1 Corinthians 2:11

Spirit of the world

Now we have received not the spirit of the world, but the Spirit which is of God, so that we might know the things that are freely given to us by God.

—1 Corinthians 2:12

Spirit of children of disobedience

In which you formerly walked according to the age of this world and according to the prince of the power of the air, the spirit who now works in the sons of disobedience.

—Ephesians 2:2

Demonic spirit

Put on the whole armor of God that you may be able to stand against the schemes of the devil. For our fight is not against flesh and blood, but against principalities, against powers, against the rulers of the darkness of this world, and against spiritual forces of evil in the heavenly places.

—Ephesians 6:11–12

But I say that the things which the Gentiles sacrifice, they sacrifice to demons, and not to God. I do not want you to have fellowship with demons. You cannot drink the cup of the Lord and the cup of demons. You cannot be partakers of the Lord's table and of the table of demons.

—1 Corinthians 10:20–21

Now the Spirit clearly says that in the last times some will depart from the faith and pay attention to seducing spirits and doctrines of devils.

—1 Timothy 4:1

Spirit of fear

For God has not given us the spirit of fear, but of power, and love, and self-control.

—2 Timothy 1:7

Spirit of error

We are of God, and whoever knows God listens to us. Whoever is not of God does not listen to us. This is how we know the spirit of truth and the spirit of error.

—1 John 4:6